HELLO HOCKEY
fans from
COAST TO COAST

HELLO HOCKEY fans from COAST TO COAST

Amazing Lists for Trivia Lovers

Jefferson **DAVIS** & Andrew **PODNIEKS**

ECW PRESS

CANADIAN CATALOGUING IN PUBLICATION DATA
Davis, Jefferson, 1962–
Hello hockey fans from coast to coast : amazing lists for trivia lovers

ISBN 1-55022-386-0

1. National Hockey League — Miscellanea. 2. Hockey — Miscellanea.
I. Podnieks, Andrew. II. Title

GV847.D394 1999   796.962   C99-93188-4

Cover and text design by Tania Craan
Layout by Mary Bowness
Printed by AGMV l'Imprimeur, Cap-Saint-Ignace, Québec

Distributed in Canada by General Distribution Services,
325 Humber Blvd., Etobicoke, Ontario M9W 7C3

Distributed in the United States by LPC Group,
1436 West Randolph Street, Chicago, Illinois, USA 60607

Published by ECW PRESS
2120 Queen Street East, Suite 200,
Toronto, Ontario, M4E 1E2
www.ecw.ca/press

The publication of *Hello Hockey Fans From Coast to Coast* has been
generously supported by the Government of Canada through the Book
Publishing Industry Development Program. Canada

PRINTED AND BOUND IN CANADA

CONTENTS

1

DECEMBER 1, 1924

Boston Bruins 2   Montreal Maroons 1

The Bruins won only five more games all season after knocking off the Maroons at the Boston Arena in the initial NHL match for both franchises. Both teams improved the following season, especially the Maroons, who went on to claim the Stanley Cup.

2

NOVEMBER 17, 1926

Chicago Blackhawks 4   Toronto St. Pats 1

The Hawks attained a respectable 41 points in 44 games in 1926–27. Although they qualified for the post-season, they were no match for the Boston Bruins. The Hawks were led by forwards Dick Irvin and Babe Dye with the former moving on to become one of the game's winningest coaches.

Dick Irvin

3

NOVEMBER 10, 1932

Detroit Red Wings 3   Chicago Blackhawks 1

After spending their initial six NHL seasons as first the Cougars and then the Falcons, the newly-named Detroit franchise earned a second-place finish in the American Division with 25 wins in 48 games. The Wings reached the semifinals later that year.

4

DECEMBER 19, 1917

Montreal Canadiens 7   Ottawa Senators 4

The Canadiens debuted in the National Hockey Association in 1910 and captured their first Stanley Cup in 1916. In their first NHL contest they outgunned Ottawa 7–4 on the strength of superstar Joe Malone's five goals. Montreal finished first in the regular season standings but didn't win their first NHL Stanley Cup until 1924.

5

NOVEMBER 16, 1926

New York Rangers 1   Montreal Maroons 0

Lorne Chabot backstopped the Blueshirts to a successful NHL debut. The team also featured Ching Johnson and Taffy Abel on defence and the "Bread Line" of Frank Boucher between Bill and Bun Cook.

6

FEBRUARY 17, 1927

Toronto Maple Leafs 4   New York Americans 1

New Owner Conn Smythe changed the Toronto team's nickname from St. Pats to Maple Leafs on Valentine's Day 1927. In their first game as the Maple Leafs, Toronto outclassed the New York Americans 4–1. The team struggled until the early 1930s when the likes of Ace Bailey, Red Horner, and the "Kid Line" of Joe Primeau, Busher Jackson, and Charlie Conacher brought the team the Stanley Cup in 1932.

Nine **MEMORABLE** Games From the NHL's **NEUTRAL-SITE EXPERIMENT** (1992-94)

1

OCTOBER 13, 1992 AT SASKATOON

Calgary Flames 4   Minnesota North Stars 3

Minnesota was technically the home team but Calgary enjoyed the ardent support of the western Canadian crowd. The North Stars outshot the Flames 27–18. Flames' defensive centre Joel Otto led the way with a goal and an assist while Mike Vernon excelled between the pipes.

2

NOVEMBER 18, 1992 AT HAMILTON

New Jersey Devils 3   Buffalo Sabres 2

The Buffalo Sabres were blamed by many Hamiltonians after Steeltown's bid for an NHL expansion franchise failed in 1991. Despite the sour atmosphere surrounding the game, the two clubs put on an entertaining show. New Jersey came from behind to win on goals by Tom Chorske and Alexandre Semak.

3

DECEMBER 8, 1992 AT PHOENIX

Montreal Canadiens 5   L.A. Kings 5

In a wild-west shootout Montreal led 2–0 after the first period. L.A. stormed back with five straight goals. Luc Robitaille's second of the game at 6:50 of the final period seemed to put the Kings in total command. Montreal charged back to tie the game when Vince Damphousse scored a natural hat trick in the last 7:40 of the third period.

4

DECEMBER 9, 1992 AT MIAMI

New York Rangers 6   Tampa Bay Lightning 5

In a game that produced a wild second period, the Rangers edged the home state Lightning 6–5. The first period ended 1–1 then the Blueshirts surged ahead 5–3. The Lightning's Brian Bradley tied the game 5–5 with his second goal. Rookie right winger Steve King had the only score of the third period to give New York the win.

5 FEBRUARY 16, 1993 AT CINCINNATI

Philadelphia Flyers 4   Calgary Flames 4

A zany first period saw the Flames take a 4–2 lead on the strength of goals by Joe Nieuwendyk, Theoren Fleury, Ronnie Stern, and Gary Roberts. The scoring slowed down during the last two-thirds of the game. Brent Fedyk tied the game in the third period. Both teams finished with 42 shots in this highly entertaining match-up.

6 FEBRUARY 22, 1993 AT CLEVELAND

Detroit Red Wings 5   Philadelphia Flyers 5

This game featured a three-goal effort by Flyers' rookie sensation Eric Lindros. Detroit took a 3–1 lead then Lindros and Greg Paslawski tied the score in the second period. The Wings led 5–3 but Brent Fedyk registered the equaliser with only one second left on the clock.

7 DECEMBER 23, 1993 AT SASKATOON

Vancouver Canucks 4   Calgary Flames 3

Saskatoon fans were treated to an exciting match between these two western Canadian rivals. Canucks diminutive forward Cliff Ronning recorded three points including the winning goal in the third period.

8 DECEMBER 26, 1993 AT ORLANDO

Florida Panthers 3   Tampa Bay Lightning 1

Intrastate rivals Florida and Tampa Bay played in Orlando with the upstart Panthers emerging victorious over their more seasoned opponent. Veteran John Vanbiesbrouck stopped 36 of 37 shots for the Panthers. On offence, Jody Hull led the way with a goal and an assist.

9 DECEMBER 31, 1993 AT MINNESOTA

Philadelphia Flyers 4   Boston Bruins 3

A year after the North Stars relocated to Dallas, nearly 11,000 Minnesota hockey fans turned out to watch Philadelphia and Boston stage a hard-fought match. Eric Lindros and Mark Recchi each had a goal and an assist for the victors.

SIX Longest UNDEFEATED STREAKS
By An NHL Team

PHILADELPHIA FLYERS 35 GAMES

1

October 14, 1979 to January 6, 1980 (25-0-10)

Following the retirement of goalie Bernie Parent, the 1979–80 Philadelphia Flyers were thought to be competitive but in transition. With coach Pat Quinn at the helm, the team was led by Stanley Cup veterans Bobby Clarke, Reggie Leach, and Bill Barber. Philadelphia surpassed the Montreal Canadiens' NHL record 28-game unbeaten streak by defeating the Boston Bruins in the Garden by a 5–2 score on December 22, 1979. The Minnesota North Stars ended the streak by clobbering Philadelphia 7–1 on January 5, 1980.

MONTREAL CANADIENS 28 GAMES

2

December 18, 1977 to February 23, 1978 (23-0-5)

After registering a record 132 points and winning their second straight Stanley Cup, the Habs put together a long undefeated streak. They were blessed with a skilled offence led by Guy Lafleur, Steve Shutt, and Jacques Lemaire, Ken Dryden in net, and a disciplined defence led by Serge Savard, Larry Robinson, and Guy Lapointe. Montreal posted 59 wins and 129 points on the way to winning their third of four consecutive Stanley Cups.

PHILADELPHIA FLYERS 23 GAMES

3

January 29 to March 18, 1976 (17-0-6)

Even though the Montreal Canadiens were the class of the NHL in 1975–76, the defending Stanley Cup champions made a statement of their own. Bobby Clarke and Bill Barber were among the NHL's leading scorers and the club continued to play an intimidating style of hockey that made them almost invincible at home.

BOSTON BRUINS 23 GAMES

4

December 22, 1940 to February 23, 1941 (15-0-8)

The Bruins had Frank Brimsek in goal, Dit Clapper led the defence, and the forwards included scoring champion Bill Cowley, Roy Conacher, and the "Kraut Line" of Woody Dumart, Milt Schmidt, and Bobby Bauer. Boston easily topped the regular season standings with a 27–8–13 record. They beat Toronto in a seven-game semifinal before sweeping past Detroit in the finals for their third Cup.

5 MONTREAL CANADIENS 21 GAMES
January 18 to March 5, 1977 (17–0–4)

The Canadiens' star-studded line-up included Lafleur, Dryden, Robinson, Gainey, Savard, Cournoyer, Lapointe, Shutt, and Lemaire. The team waltzed through the regular season recording an NHL record 132 points before winning their second straight Stanley Cup with a four-game sweep of Boston.

6 NEW YORK RANGERS 19 GAMES
November 23, 1939 to January 13, 1940 (14–0–5)

The Rangers put together their greatest streak the year they won their last Stanley Cup for over five decades. This was a well-balanced roster that finished a close second to Boston in the regular season standings but allowed the fewest goals in the league. Netminder Dave Kerr posted a league low 1.60 goals against average while Bryan Hextall, Neal and Mac Colville, Alex Shibicky, Clint Smith, and Murray Patrick were some of the key contributors to the team's success.

Pete Peeters in goal for the Flyers.

Eight **LARGEST POINT** Increases By An NHL Team In Its **SECOND** Season

1

BOSTON BRUINS +26
1924 25 to 1925-26

In their first NHL season the Bruins finished with six wins and 24 losses in 30 matches leaving them 27 points behind the first-place Hamilton Tigers. The next year they posted a decent 17–15–4 record for 38 points and a fourth place finish out of seven teams.

2

N.Y. ISLANDERS +26
1972–73 to 1973-74

In their first year the New York Islanders suffered through a dreadful 30-point season and lost 60 of their 78 games. The next year they improved to 56 points led by Calder Trophy winning defenceman Denis Potvin and coach Al Arbour. In their third NHL season the Islanders made the playoffs, losing to the Philadelphia Flyers in seven games in the semifinals.

3

MONTREAL MAROONS +25
1924–25 to 1925-26

The Maroons began play in 1924–25 and won only nine of 30 games to finish 16 points behind their arch rivals, the Canadiens. In 1925–26 the team finished in second place and defeated Pittsburgh, Ottawa, and the WHL's Victoria Cougars on the way to the Stanley Cup. They were led by NHL scoring champion Nels Stewart, Punch Broadbent, Babe Siebert, and netminder Clint Benedict.

4

OAKLAND/CALIFORNIA SEALS +22
1967–68 to 1968-69

After finishing last among the six expansion clubs in 1967–68, the Seals improved by 22 points and jumped to second place in the West Division standings. Their improvement was partly attributable to the addition of Carol Vadnais, Bobby Baun, and Bryan Watson on defence along with netminders Charlie Hodge and Gary Smith.

5

ST. LOUIS BLUES +18
1967–68 to 1968–69

The St. Louis Blues increased from 70 to 88 points in their sophomore NHL season. In both years they played well in the playoffs and reached the Stanley Cup finals. Blues fans were fortunate to catch stars Glenn Hall, Jacques Plante, Doug Harvey, and Dickie Moore at the end of their NHL careers.

6

TAMPA BAY LIGHTNING +18
1992–93 to 1993–94

During their first NHL season, the Lightning accumulated a respectable 53 points. In 1993–94 they narrowly missed the playoffs by registering 71 points. The strength of the team was sound defence and disciplined play stressed by coach Terry Crisp.

7

QUEBEC NORDIQUES +17
1979–80 to 1980–81

The Nordiques entered the NHL from the WHA with much of their line-up unchanged, but a rash of injuries late in the season caused the club to finish with just 61 points. The following season the team added Peter and Anton Stastny and young forward Dale Hunter, and received more production from Michel Goulet. Another factor in the team's 78-point total was fiery coach Michel Bergeron's motivational power.

8

DETROIT COUGARS +16
1926–27 to 1927–28

The Detroit Cougars (later known as the Red Wings) debuted in 1926–27 with a 12–28–4 record. The addition of Jack Adams as general manager paid dividends. The team played with renewed vigour in their second season and finished with 44 points in as many games. They finished only three points behind the eventual Stanley Cup champion New York Rangers.

FIVE Most Lopsided **STANLEY** Cup-Winning Games (since 1918)

1

APRIL 1, 1920

Ottawa Senators 6   Seattle Metropolitans 1

The best-of-five series began in Ottawa, but mild weather created poor rink conditions and the games were moved to Toronto where artificial ice could be used. The teams split the first four games, and in the decisive fifth Jack Darragh's hat trick lifted the Senators to an easy win over the Metropolitans.

2

MARCH 30, 1925

Victoria Cougars 6   Montreal Canadiens 1

The Cougars were the last non-NHL team to win the Cup. The team featured Harry Holmes in goal, Frank Fredrickson at centre, and Harry Meeking up front. A 1–0 lead after the first period erupted into a 5–1 lead after two, and the Habs' goalie was no match for the western team.

3

APRIL 14, 1948

Toronto Maple Leafs 7   Detroit Red Wings 2

This was the middle Cup victory of the first-ever three in a row, and it was accomplished with all the team's greatest stars of the era. Toronto went up 3–0 in the first on goals by Ted Kennedy, Garth Boesch, and Harry Watson, and added three more in the second to continue the rout.

MAY 30, 1985

Edmonton Oilers 8   Philadelphia Flyers 3

The Oilers, sparked by Paul Coffey's two goals, were up 4–1 in the first before the Flyers got their legs warm. Two goals by Gretzky and one by Mark Messier in the second gave goalie Grant Fuhr a comfortable lead with which to work.

MAY 25, 1991

Pittsburgh Penguins 8   Minnesota North Stars 0

The greatest Cup-deciding whitewash of all, with Mario Lemieux at the height of his powers. Lemieux had a goal and three assists, and the Pens scored three times in each of the first two periods to coast to the silverware. Tom Barrasso got the shutout, and amazingly he faced more shots than Jon Casey and Brian Hayward at the other end (39 to 28).

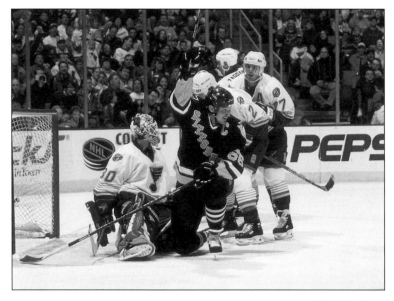

Mario Lemieux

Four Memorable **COMEBACKS** in a **PLAYOFF** Game

1

APRIL 17, 1977
Philadelphia 6   Toronto 5 (OT)

Philadelphia won series 4–2. During the 1977 quarterfinals
the Toronto Maple Leafs won the first two games at the Philadelphia
Spectrum. A fourth-game comeback reversed the momentum in the
series. Toronto led 5–2 in the third period courtesy of Lanny
McDonald's four-goal performance. The Flyers refused to give up
and Reggie Leach scored at 19:10 of the extra period to tie the
series. Toronto never recovered.

2

APRIL 10, 1982
Los Angeles 6   Edmonton 5 (OT)

Los Angeles won series 3–2. During the regular season
Edmonton finished 48 points ahead of L.A., a record margin for
playoff combatants. The upstart Kings won the third match 6–5 to
take a 2 games to 1 lead. Edmonton held a 5–0 lead after two periods before L.A. struck back to send the game into overtime. Daryl
Evans scored the winner at 2:35 of the overtime.

3

APRIL 5, 1983
Boston 4   Quebec 3 (OT)

Boston won series 3–1. Peter Stastny scored a hat trick in the
first period to give his team a 3–0 lead. Boston fought back to force
overtime then Barry Pederson scored at 1:46 of the first overtime.
They won both games at home then split two contests at the Colisée
to eliminate the Nordiques.

4

MAY 26, 1992
Pittsburgh 5   Chicago 4

Pittsburgh won series 4–0. The defending Stanley Cup champion Pittsburgh Penguins entered the 1992 Final against a Chicago
team that was on an eleven-game winning streak. Chicago took a
3–0 lead in the first period and led 4–1 in the second period when
the Pens started playing like champions. Jaromir Jagr tied the game
late in the game. The Hawks continued to battle throughout the
series but they were never the same after this initial loss.

Ten Most **LOPSIDED** Playoff Series
VICTORIES (seven-game series)

1

DETROIT VS. SAN JOSE, 1995

This was a little payback for the Wings, who had been eliminated by the surprising Sharks in seven games the previous year. The Wings won 6–0 and 6–2 in Detroit before closing the "modern tennis" match with two more 6–2 wins.

2

RANGERS VS. ISLANDERS, 1994

For a while, this series wasn't about who would win but about whether the Islanders were ever going to score. The Rangers won the first two games 6–0, then hammered the Isles on Long Island 5–1 and 5–2 on their way to their first Cup win in fifty years.

3

MONTREAL VS. ST. LOUIS, 1977

The Blues were victims to Montreal, scoring only four goals and allowing 19 in the quarterfinal series. Montreal won by scores of 7–2, 3–0, 5–1, and 4–1 en route to their second of four successive Stanley Cup wins.

4

BOSTON VS. ST. LOUIS, 1972

After beating Minnesota in seven games in the quarterfinals, the Blues ran up against the powerful Bruins and were hammered in four straight. Boston won 6–1 and 10–2 at home, then finished the job in St. Louis with wins of 7–2 and 5–3. Not even close.

5

BOSTON VS. TORONTO, 1969

This marked the end of the Punch Imlach era in Toronto and the start of the Bruins' domination, led by Bobby Orr. The Beantowners crushed the Leafs 10–0 and 7–0 at home, then won in Toronto by scores of 4–3 and 3–2.

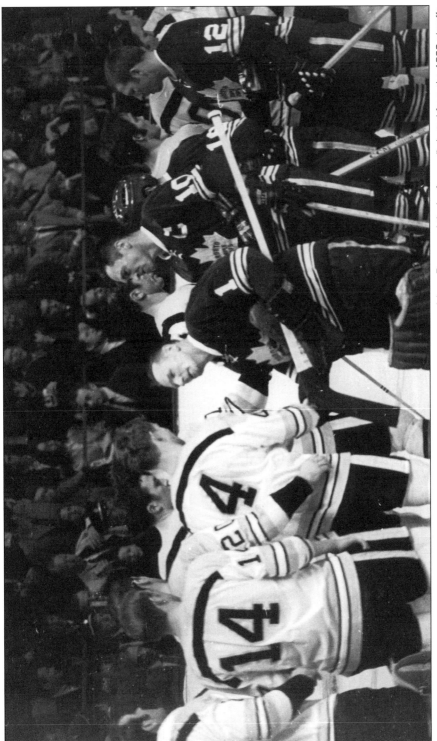

Johnny Bower and the Leafs are eliminated from the 1969 playoffs.

6   MONTREAL VS. DETROIT, 1958

The Habs were in the middle of their unmatched five-Cup dynasty while the Wings were just ending their incredible success of the early 1950s. This series was no contest, the Habs winning at home 8–1 and 5–1, then 2–1 and 4–3 at the Olympia in Detroit.

7   MONTREAL VS. BOSTON, 1954

Although they were close in the standings, the Bruins were no match for Montreal in this semifinals series. Montreal won the first game 2–0 and followed with an 8–1 hammering before travelling to Boston for the last two games of the series. In the Garden, Montreal won 4–3, then ended the match-up as they began, with a 2–0 whitewash.

8   DETROIT VS. MONTREAL, 1952

Arguably the finest Detroit team ever assembled by Jack Adams, the Wings thoroughly overpowered Montreal to win the Cup in 1952, despite not having home ice advantage. They won the first two games at the Forum, 3–1 and 2–1; the Habs lost the last two 3–0 in Detroit.

9   MONTREAL VS. BOSTON, 1946

With all their players back from war, Montreal was too good for Boston in the first round of the playoffs. Montreal won 6–2, 5–1, 8–2, and 7–2 to set a record for most goals in a four-game finals series. The record wasn't broken until Boston scored 28 in 1972 vs. St. Louis.

10   MONTREAL VS. TORONTO, 1944

Toronto took one game in this series, but the other four weren't close. The Leafs won the opening game 3–1 in Montreal, but the Habs rebounded with a 5–1 win at the Forum, and both games at the Gardens, 2–1 and 4–1. The Habs set a record for most goals in a playoff game by eliminating the Leafs 11–0 in Montreal.

Eight **WORST REGULAR SEASON** **RECORDS** By a Stanley Cup Champion

1

1937-38 CHICAGO BLACKHAWKS [14-25-9]

A mild upset over the Montreal Canadiens was followed by a stunning victory over the New York Americans. Chicago completed its Cinderella story by defeating the much-fancied Toronto Maple Leafs in the finals.

2

1948-49 TORONTO MAPLE LEAFS [22-25-13]

The defending Stanley Cup champions finished a distant fourth in the NHL's regular season. They pushed aside Boston in the semifinals before shocking the Detroit Red Wings in the final series. Sid Smith's hat trick in the second game sent Toronto home with a 2–0 series lead. Detroit dropped the last two games of the final by identical 3–1 scores.

3

1944-45 TORONTO MAPLE LEAFS [24-22-5]

The Maple Leafs exceeded all expectations by eliminating the powerhouse Habs in a six-game semifinal. Toronto capped its storybook post-season by edging Detroit in seven games. Teeder Kennedy, Babe Pratt, and Bob Davidson shone in the final during which Toronto built a 3–0 series lead. The Wings captured the next three contests and seemed poised to gain revenge on Toronto for the famous comeback of 1941–42. Babe Pratt scored the dramatic Cup-winner to ensure his club its second title of the 1940s.

4

1923-24 MONTREAL CANADIENS [13–11–0]

Montreal completed the regular season well back of the first-place Senators. After stunning Ottawa in the NHL championship series, the Canadiens disposed of the PCHA-champion Vancouver Millionaires. They then dominated the Western Canada League champion Calgary Tigers by scores of 6–1 and 3–0 in the two-game playoff. Howie Morenz dazzled while scoring a hat trick in the first game and Georges Vézina posted a shutout in the Cup-clinching match.

5   1921-22 TORONTO ST. PATS [13-10-1]

After finishing second in the NHL standings with an unspectacular 27 points, Toronto startled the favoured Ottawa Senators in the post-season then faced the Western Canada Hockey League champion Vancouver Millionaires for the Stanley Cup. Toronto fell behind two games to one in the best-of-five series before claiming the last two contests by an aggregate score of 11–1.

6   1927-28 NEW YORK RANGERS [19-16-9]

The Broadway Blueshirts topped the Pittsburgh Pirates, then defeated the favoured Boston Bruins before facing the powerful Montreal Maroons in the final. The Maroons won the opening contest before the series turned in game two. In that contest, New York's 45-year-old coach Lester Patrick was pressed into action when starting netminder Lorne Chabot was injured.

7   1933-34 CHICAGO BLACKHAWKS [20-17-11]

The Chicago Blackhawks jelled at the appropriate time to win their first Stanley Cup. They bested the Montreal Canadiens, and then the Maroons, before upsetting Detroit in the final. The Hawks were led by Chuck Gardiner's heroic goalkeeping, Lionel Conacher and Taffy Abel's rugged play on defence, and the timely offensive contributions of Paul Thompson and Mush March.

8   1994-95 NEW JERSEY DEVILS [22-18-8]

The 1994–95 NHL regular season was reduced to 48 games as a result of a four-month lockout. New Jersey went through an unremarkable regular season which placed them fifth in the Eastern Conference. They disposed of Boston, Pittsburgh, and Philadelphia before capturing the Stanley Cup with a four-games-to-one victory over Detroit. The Devils were led by the goal scoring of Conn Smythe Trophy winner Claude Lemieux.

Ten Regular Season **CHAMPS** to be **KNOCKED OUT** in the **FIRST ROUND** of the Playoffs (pre-1967)

1

DETROIT RED WINGS 1964-65

In the pre-expansion NHL, the playoff match-ups were decided by pitting the first-place team against the third, and the second against the fourth. First-place Detroit played third-place Chicago in 1965, and the Hawks prevailed 4–2 in game seven of their series. Bobby Hull, who led the postseason in scoring, was the only player to score ten goals in the playoffs.

2

MONTREAL CANADIENS 1963-64

Although the Leafs finished third to Montreal's first, only seven points and three wins separated them in the standings, and in Montreal the Leafs eliminated the Habs and went on to win their third successive Cup. Johnny Bower was phenomenal in the nets for Toronto, and the "Big M," Frank Mahovlich, led the team in scoring with 15 points.

3

MONTREAL CANADIENS 1961-62

When the Hawks beat the Habs in the first round of the playoffs, a significant upset had occurred. Chicago finished 23 points behind the Habs in the regular season, but goalie Jacques Plante was no match for Bobby Hull who led the league in goals (50) and points (84) and was key to his team's victory.

4

MONTREAL CANADIENS 1960-61

Having won a phenomenal five Stanley Cups in a row, Montreal finished first in the regular-season standings and seemed destined to win a sixth. Each team won once at home and once on the road. With the series tied 2–2, the Hawks took over, winning the last two games by 3–0 shutouts.

5 DETROIT RED WINGS 1956-57

After winning the opening game of the series 3–1 in Detroit, the Bruins were thrashed 7–2 in game two. The mighty Wings looked like they were on their way to victory. But the big line of Lindsay-Howe-Ullman could do no more damage. Detroit lost the next three games 4–3, 2–0, and 4–3, and were eliminated in a humbling five games.

6 DETROIT RED WINGS 1952-53

There were two mini-turning points in the Detroit-Boston first-round match-up. The first came in game two in Detroit. After being hammered 7–0 in the opener, Boston managed to fight back for a 5–3 win. The Bruins won game three 2–1 in overtime and won their next home game. While Detroit won game five 6–4 in Detroit, the Bruins won 4–2 at the Garden to eliminate the Stanley Cup champions in six games.

7 DETROIT RED WINGS 1950-51

The Toronto-Montreal final was set up when the Habs beat the defending Cup champion Red Wings in six games. Montreal had finished 36 points behind the Wings in the standings but won the first two games of the series in Detroit, both in overtime, to set up their 3–2 win in game six.

8 MONTREAL CANADIENS 1944-45

Montreal went 38–8–4 during the regular season, and Toronto's record was 24–22–4, but it was the Leafs, backed by goaler Frank McCool, who eliminated the Habs in six games. The turning point came in game four. Toronto had swept both games in Montreal, but the Habs rebounded to win the first game in Maple Leaf Gardens. Toronto scored in overtime of game four to take a commanding 3–1 lead in games, but Montreal came back with a crushing 10–3 win. The loss was easily forgotten by the Leafs, who won 3–2 in Toronto to advance to the finals.

NEW YORK RANGERS 1941-42

The top two teams, Toronto and New York, played in the first round, the winner advancing to the finals. The third-place team played the fourth, and the fifth played sixth, and the two winners played each other to fill the other spot in the finals. Game one was played in Toronto, games two and three in New York, four and six in Toronto and five in New York. The Leafs won the sixth game 3–2 and went on to win the Cup by defeating Detroit after trailing 3–0 in the series.

BOSTON BRUINS 1939-40

10

This was perhaps the finest Bruins team of all time, with Dumart, Schmidt, and Bauer on forward, Dit Clapper and Flash Hollett on defence, and Frankie Brimsek in goal. But the Rangers, who were just three points the weaker in the standings, beat the Bruins 4–1 in game six and advanced to the finals where they beat the Leafs in six.

Montreal vs. Toronto at Maple Leaf Gardens.

1

DAN BAIN   JANUARY 31, 1901
Winnipeg Victorias 2   Montreal Shamrocks 1

The first Stanley Cup-clinching goal in overtime was registered by the Winnipeg Victorias' legendary Dan Bain. A gifted centre and on-ice leader, Bain was chosen Canada's outstanding athlete of the 19th century. He was among the initial group of players elected to the Hockey Hall of Fame in 1945.

2

BILL COOK   APRIL 13, 1933
New York Rangers 1   Toronto Maple Leafs 0

The NHL's first Cup-winning goal in overtime was recorded by star right-winger Bill Cook. The Blueshirts' victory was accomplished even though the circus forced them out of Madison Square Garden and into Toronto's Maple Leaf Gardens for the last three games of the final.

3

MUSH MARCH   APRIL 10, 1934
Chicago Blackhawks 1   Detroit Red Wings 0

Chicago's first Stanley Cup depended on a goal by Harold "Mush" March, which lifted the Hawks to a 3–1 series triumph over Detroit in their first of two championship seasons in the 1930s.

4

BRYAN HEXTALL   APRIL 13, 1940
New York Rangers 3   Toronto Maple Leafs 2

Talented right-winger Bryan Hextall fired the overtime winner that brought the Rangers their third Stanley Cup title. He earned a place on the NHL First All-Star team that year and in 1969 was elected to the Hockey Hall of Fame.

TOE BLAKE   APRIL 13, 1944

Montreal Canadiens 5   Chicago Blackhawks 4

Montreal left-winger Toe Blake was the overtime hero as the Canadiens swept the Chicago Blackhawks to claim the Cup. Blake formed the dangerous "Punch Line" with fellow Hockey Hall of Fame members Maurice Richard and Elmer Lach. The contest was also known for Bill Durnan's save on Virgil Johnson, the first penalty shot in the history of the finals.

PETE BABANDO   APRIL 23, 1950

Detroit Red Wings 4   New York Rangers 3

Pete Babando delivered the Cup-winning tally in the seventh game as the Red Wings won their first of four titles in the early 1950s. The series against the Rangers was closer than expected because Red Wing Gordie Howe was seriously hurt in the semifinal against Toronto and Don Raleigh scored two OT winners for the Blueshirts in the final.

BILL BARILKO   APRIL 21, 1951

Toronto Maple Leafs 3   Montreal Canadiens 2

In one of hockey's best-remembered scenes, Toronto defenceman Bill Barilko scored the dramatic Cup-winning goal in a final where all five games went into extra time. Sadly, a few weeks after his heroics, he lost his life in a plane crash. The Maple Leafs capped the most successful period in franchise history with their fifth triumph in seven seasons.

ELMER LACH   APRIL 16, 1953

Montreal Canadiens 1   Boston Bruins 0

Centre Elmer Lach scored in overtime of the fifth game of the finals. Of interest was the replacement of goalie Jacques Plante with Gerry McNeil for the last three games of the series. McNeil had two shutouts against the Bruins.

9   TONY LESWICK   APRIL 16, 1954

Detroit Red Wings 2   Montreal Canadiens 1

The early 1950s were characterised by a fierce rivalry between Montreal and Detroit. Wings forward Tony Leswick scored the overtime winner in the seventh and deciding game which brought Motown its third title of the decade.

10   HENRI RICHARD   MAY 5, 1966

Montreal Canadiens 3   Detroit Red Wings 2

The "Pocket Rocket" Henri Richard scored in overtime to vault the Montreal Canadiens to a 4–2 series win and their second consecutive Stanley Cup. The Wings captured the first two games in Montreal before the Habs rallied to win the last four.

11   BOBBY ORR   MAY 10, 1970

Boston Bruins 4   St. Louis Blues 3

By scoring likely the most famous overtime goal in league history, superstar defenceman Bobby Orr ended a Bruins Stanley Cup drought that dated back to 1940–41. The historic marker came at the expense of the legendary Glenn Hall, who was lured out of retirement to play for the expansion Blues in 1967–68.

12   JACQUES LEMAIRE   MAY 14, 1977

Montreal Canadiens 2   Boston Bruins 1

Habs' centre Jacques Lemaire scored in overtime to give his squad a four-game sweep over the Boston Bruins. His goal was the pinnacle of the most dominant single season by an NHL team as the Habs posted a 60–8–12 record for 132 points. This was the second of four straight Cup wins for the Canadiens.

13   BOB NYSTROM   MAY 24, 1980

New York Islanders 5   Philadelphia Flyers 4

Bob Nystrom ushered in a new era by scoring the overtime winner that gave the Islanders their first of four consecutive Stanley Cups. Nystrom was one of the most proficient overtime scorers in history. The Islanders became the second expansion franchise to win the Stanley Cup after Philadelphia's consecutive triumphs in 1974 and 1975.

14   UWE KRUPP   JUNE 10, 1996

Colorado Avalanche 1   Florida Panthers 0

Defenceman Uwe Krupp ended the longest 1–0 game in the history of the finals when he scored four and a half minutes into the third extra period to give Colorado a four-game sweep over upstart Florida. The Avalanche reached the peak of hockey success in their first year after leaving Quebec City for Denver.

15   BRETT HULL   JUNE 19, 1999

Dallas Stars 2   Buffalo Sabres 1

Right-winger Brett Hull delivered Dallas' first Stanley Cup at 15:41 of the third overtime period. The Stars defeated the Buffalo Sabres in a hotly contested six-game final to become the last Stanley Cup Champions of the 20th century.

Bill Barilko scores the Cup-winning goal.

23

PLAYERS To WIN The Stanley Cup With The MOST TEAMS

1   **JACK MARSHALL, 4**

Marshall never played in the NHL but still made it into the Hockey Hall of Fame, thanks in large measure to his incredible playoff success wherever he went. He won Cups with the Winnipeg Vics in 1901, the Montreal AAA the next year, and the Montreal Wanderers in 1907 and 1910. He finished his great Cup-career with the Blueshirts, winning in 1914 with Toronto.

2   **AL ARBOUR, 3**

A bespectacled journeyman defenceman, Arbour played more in the minors than the NHL during his career. Although he didn't play in the 1954 playoffs with Detroit, his 36 regular season games got his name on the '54 Red Wings Cup. In Chicago, he played most of the 1960–61 season and won with the Leafs the following year. In 1963–64 he played just six regular season games and one in the playoffs for Toronto, but that was good enough for another name engraving on the Cup, his fourth with his third team.

3   **FRANK FOYSTON, 3**

Foyston played hockey for 20 years, but only two seasons in the NHL. He played with the Blueshirts from 1912 to 1916 and was Jack Marshall's teammate for that 1914 Cup win. He then played with the Seattle Metropolitans for nine years, winning the Cup in 1917, and finally with the Victoria Cougars in 1925.

4   **LARRY HILLMAN, 3**

Hillman was another player to spend as much time in the minor leagues as in the NHL. When the Wings won the Cup in 1955, he played just six regular season games and three more in the playoffs. With Toronto, he played from 1960–68, but was in the minors every year but the first. Still, he qualified for name engraving in both 1964 and 1967 with the Leafs and won another Cup with Montreal in 1969 after being traded mid-season from Minnesota.

Jack Walker

5   HARRY HOLMES, 3

Like Foyston, Holmes was perfectly content playing hockey outside the NHL, and in nearly 20 years of tending the goal, he played just 103 games in the National League. He won the Cup with both early Toronto teams, the Blueshirts in 1914 and the Arenas in 1918, and was Foyston's teammate for the 1917 Seattle triumph and again for the 1925 Victoria win.

6   MIKE KEANE, 3

The most recent name, Keane not only has won three Cups with different teams but all in the 1990s and all, curiously, "pregnant 3s" as they say in poker parlance. He won in 1993 with the surprising Montreal Canadiens, 1996 with the dominant Colorado Avalanche, and 1999 with the Dallas Stars.

7   CLAUDE LEMIEUX, 3

A recent addition to this rare group, Lemieux won Cups with Montreal in 1986, New Jersey in 1995, and Colorado the next year. He is also the only member of this list to win the Conn Smythe Trophy (initiated in 1964–65) during the Devils' run to the Cup.

8   GORD PETTINGER, 3

Pettinger won four Cups with three teams in just seven years, starting with the Rangers in 1933, his NHL rookie season. After the win, he was traded to the Red Wings and won back-to-back Cups with Detroit in 1936 and 1937. Midway through the following season he was sent to Boston, and in 1939 he won the hallowed hardware with the Bruins.

9   JACK WALKER, 3

Like many others, notably Marshall, Holmes, and Foyston in this list, Walker spent most of his years in the Pacific Coast and Western leagues. He was on the magical troika of teams that won Stanley Cups with non-NHL teams — 1914 Blueshirts, 1917 Metropolitans, and 1925 Cougars.

Ten LONGEST-SERVING NHL CAPTAINS

1

STEVE YZERMAN

Yzerman became captain of the Detroit Red Wings to start the 1986–87 season, replacing Danny Gare, who signed with the Oilers. It was Yzerman's fourth year with the Red Wings, and he is now in his fourteenth season as captain, having played more than 1,000 games with the "C" on his Winged Wheel sweater.

2

GEORGE ARMSTRONG

"Army" succeeded Ted Kennedy as captain of the Leafs to start the 1957–58 season and remained team leader through the '68–'69 season, some 12 years and nearly 800 games. He won four Stanley Cups as captain, and although he retired at season's end, by which time Dave Keon was named his replacement, he later returned to play another two seasons with the Blue and White.

3

PIERRE PILOTE

Pilote captained the Chicago Blackhawks from 1961–68, replacing Ed Litzenberger, and won three Norris Trophies during his captaincy. He played his entire 890-game NHL career in Chicago — except his final season when he was with Toronto — and was 30 years old when he was given the "C" by the Hawks.

4

ALEX DELVECCHIO

Another great Red Wing of an earlier era, "Fats" served as Detroit's leader for an incredible eleven seasons, 1962–73, and part of the next year before he retired to take over as coach of the team. He played all of his 24 years in the league with the Wings, a league record for service with one team, winning three Cups during his pre-captain years.

5

JEAN BELIVEAU

"Le Gros Bil" was captain of the Habs for a decade, 1961–71, and took over the leader's role from Doug Harvey after Harvey went to the New York Rangers as player/coach. Beliveau won ten Stanley Cups with Montreal, five while captain, and ceased his tenure as captain only when he retired.

6

BOB GAINEY

Gainey was another lifelong member of the Habs and was for many years considered the best two-way player in the game. He was captain from 1981–89, a stretch of nearly 600 games. He won one Cup while wearing the "C" after a run of four in the late seventies under predecessors Yvan Cournoyer and Serge Savard.

7

BILL COOK

Cook was the Rangers' first captain, when the team entered the league in 1926, and lasted in that position for every game of his NHL career. He is the only player in league history to play his first NHL game as team captain, and his reign lasted for eleven years and 474 games.

8

BRIAN SUTTER

It took Brian Sutter just three years to become the St. Louis Blues' team captain in 1979, a position he held until his retirement some nine years later. The first of six Sutter-playing brothers to make it to the NHL, Brian was also one of four to become captains (along with Ron in Philadelphia, Brent with the Islanders, and Darryl with Chicago).

9

HAPPY DAY

Happy Day became the first captain of the Toronto Maple Leafs in 1927–28 after the team changed names from the St. Pats the previous season. He stayed leader for ten years, during which time the team won one Stanley Cup and made it to the finals three other times. Day became the first man in the NHL to win the Stanley Cup as player, coach, and general manager.

10

STAN SMYL

Smyl captained the Vancouver Canucks from 1982–90, bringing long-term stability to a position that had seen five captains the previous eleven years. Smyl played one final year with the Canucks while three others alternated in the role (Dan Quinn, Doug Lidster, and Trevor Linden), and in honour of his outstanding 13-year Vancouver career his number 12 was retired after he retired, in 1991.

FIRST Ten CAPTAINS Of The New Jersey DEVILS Franchise

1
SIMON NÔLET

Nôlet was claimed by Kansas City at the Expansion Draft in 1974 after seven seasons with the Flyers and was immediately installed as the franchise's first captain. He played only a season and a half with the Scouts before being traded to Pittsburgh. At the end of the year, the Scouts moved to Colorado and became the Rockies, and the new team reacquired Nôlet and made him captain again for one year before he retired.

2
WILF PAIEMENT

Paiement was Kansas City's first choice (second overall) in the 1974 amateur draft and made the team that fall at his first camp. After Nolet retired, Paiement was elected captain for the next year, and though Gary Croteau was captain the year after, Paiement remained with the Rockies for another year and a half before being traded to Toronto in a blockbuster deal that brought another eventual captain, Lanny McDonald, to Denver.

3
GARY CROTEAU

Croteau was a senior member of the Rockies by the time he was made captain for the '78–'79 season. He was selected by Kansas City at the expansion draft in 1974 and had been with the team ever since but played only 15 games the following season before ending his NHL career.

4
MIKE CHRISTIE

One of three captains for 1979–80, Christie had been acquired by Colorado the previous year from Cleveland for Dennis O'Brien. A big, solid defenceman, he never scored much but was considered a leader in the dressing room. Early the following season, he was sold outright to Vancouver.

RENÉ ROBERT

5 Robert was acquired at the start of the 1980–81 season from Buffalo, where he starred with the "French Connection" line for years. The Devils gave up John Van Boxmeer to get Robert, but like Paiement, he was traded to Toronto midway through the following season.

LANNY McDONALD

6 McDonald was Colorado's first franchise player, a proven all-star, a scorer of the first order, and a popular man in the dressing room. He inherited the captaincy from Robert and remained designated team leader until the day he was traded, to Calgary, two years later. In his only full season in Colorado, he had 35 goals and 81 points.

Lanny McDonald

7 ROB RAMAGE

Ramage was captain for Colorado's last year in that city before the club moved to New Jersey in the summer of 1982. At the tender age of 21, he was starting his third season in the NHL after being drafted first overall by the Rockies in 1979. He was traded to St. Louis at the end of the year for a first-round draft choice (John MacLean) and played another dozen years in the NHL.

8 DON LEVER

Lever arrived in Colorado as part of the Lanny McDonald trade with Calgary and was named the New Jersey Devils' first captain. He held the job by himself for a year and then shared duties the following season with Mel Bridgman. Just prior to the start of the '85–'86 season, he was traded to Buffalo.

9 MEL BRIDGMAN

Bridgman was the prototypical leader, a man cut from the same cloth as longtime Philadelphia teammate Bobby Clarke. A first overall selection at the 1975 draft, Bridgman played nearly seven years with Clarke before going to Calgary and then New Jersey. Before Kirk Muller, he was the franchise's longest-serving captain.

10 KIRK MULLER

Chosen second overall in the 1984 entry draft, Muller was another successful draft choice to make it big with the team. He made the team that fall, and after a three-year apprenticeship under Bridgman, was made captain to start the 1987–88 season. He remained team leader until he was traded to the Canadiens just before the start of the '91–'92 season.

RUSS BLINCO

Montreal Maroons   1934

Russ Blinco was a solid centre who won the top rookie award in 1934 after scoring 23 points in 31 games for the Montreal Maroons. The next year he helped the franchise win its second and last Stanley Cup. Following the disbanding of the Maroons in 1938, Blinco played one more year with Chicago and retired with 125 points in 268 regular season matches.

JACK GELINEAU

Boston Bruins   1950

Following in the footsteps of Frank Brimsek, McGill University graduate Jack Gelineau won 22 games and the Calder Trophy in 1950. In 1950–51 he led all NHL netminders with 70 appearances but only played two more NHL games after losing his job to Sugar Jim Henry in 1951.

PENTTI LUND

New York Rangers   1949

Lund was the first Finnish born player to win a major NHL trophy when he captured the Calder in 1949. He originally belonged to Boston but was traded to the Rangers where he scored 30 points in 59 games his rookie year. During his second year, Lund scored 11 points in 12 playoff games. He returned briefly to Boston before retiring after the 1952–53 season with 44 goals and 99 points in 259 regular season matches.

KILBY MacDONALD

New York Rangers   1940

Left-winger Kilby MacDonald's 28 points in 44 games for the Stanley Cup champion New York Rangers earned him the Calder Trophy. He experienced the "sophomore jinx" in 1940–41 with only 11 points then spent a year in the AHL. He retired in 1945 with only 70 career points.

JIM McFADDEN

Detroit Red Wings   1948

A solid NHL performer from the late 1940s to the mid-1950s, Jim McFadden won the Calder Trophy after producing an impressive 24 goals and 48 points in 1947–48. He was traded to Chicago where he spent two and a half seasons before retiring with 226 career points.

JOHN QUILTY

Montreal Canadiens   1941

Centre John Quilty lasted only two full NHL seasons, one of which saw him score 34 points and win the Calder Trophy. From 1942 to 1944 he played with RCAF teams then moved into full military service in 1944–45. After the war Quilty played 29 games with Montreal and Boston before ending his NHL career in 1948 with 70 total points.

LARRY REGAN

Boston Bruins   1957

Right-winger Larry Regan earned the Calder Trophy after his 33-point performance for the Boston Bruins in 1956–57. He set a personal high of 39 points in his second term but tailed off in subsequent years. Regan ended his NHL career in 1961 after totalling 136 points in 280 games.

BRIT SELBY

Toronto Maple Leafs   1966

Brit Selby was a key figure on the Toronto Marlboros' Memorial Cup win in 1964. His 27 points for the Maple Leafs in 1965–66 earned him the Calder Trophy. After that he became a role player for Toronto, Philadelphia, and St. Louis before moving on to the WHA in 1972–73. Selby accumulated 55 goals and 117 points in 350 regular season contests in the NHL.

ERIC VAIL

9

Atlanta Flames   1975

Claimed 21st overall in the 1973 Amateur Draft by the Atlanta
Flames, Vail won the Calder Trophy in 1975 after scoring 39 goals
in 72 games. He scored at least 20 goals five straight years for
Atlanta/Calgary from 1976–77 to 1980–81. Vail retired with 216
goals in 591 regular season games.

GRANT WARWICK

10

New York Rangers   1942

After scoring 33 points in 44 games for the 1941–42 New York
Rangers, right-winger Grant Warwick was presented the Calder
Trophy. He was a dependable scorer who reached the 20-goal mark
on three occasions. He retired in 1950 after scoring 147 goals and
289 points.

THE ORIGINAL
CORK SCREW
WITH THE THOUSAND
STICKS AND SEVEN
LEAGUE BOOTS
AND SKATES
ALSO AN ADAM'S APPLE –

Ten Best **HART TROPHY** Runners-Up
Who **NEVER WON**

SYL APPS

1

Apps is the only man never to win the Hart who was runner-up three times — 1939, 1940, and 1942. One of the greatest players of all time, he is a member of the Hockey Hall of Fame and played all his ten years in the NHL with the Leafs. One of the finest Canadians of this century, he passed away December 26, 1998.

BILL COOK

2

Twice runner-up (to Herb Gardiner in 1927 and Eddie Shore in 1933), Bill played in the NHL with brothers Bun and Bud on the "Bread Line" but is the only one of the three not elected into the Hockey Hall of Fame. He played with the Rangers all eleven years of his career, winning the Stanley Cup twice, in '28 and '33.

LIONEL CONACHER

3

Another double runner-up, the "Big Train" played 12 years in the NHL and was elected into the Hockey Hall of Fame in 1994 as a veteran player. He was named Canada's greatest athlete of the first half of the century.

BILL DURNAN

4

He wasn't the first goalie to be runner-up, but he was one of 16 to finish second in the voting over the years. Durnan was an ambidextrous goalie. In the days of two-gloved keepers, he would shift his stick from hand to hand as play moved from one side of the ice to the other. He played just seven full seasons for the Canadiens, winning two Cups and four times, playing every minute of every game of a season.

RED KELLY

5

Perhaps the greatest unsung player of all time, Kelly was runner-up to goaler Al Rollins in Hart Trophy voting for 1954. He won eight Stanley Cups, four each with Detroit and Toronto. He was a great defenceman and centre and was selected to all-star teams at both positions. In 1967, after 20 seasons in the league, Kelly became head coach of the expansion Los Angeles Kings.

Red Kelly wearing the "C" for a game.

6 JOHNNY BOWER

Bower's career began after 13 seasons in the minors, punctuated by one year with the Rangers in '53–'54. He joined the Leafs in 1958 and went on to play for another decade, win four Stanley Cups, and establish himself as one of the greatest goalers of all time. He was Hart runner-up to Montreal's Boom Boom Geoffrion in 1961.

7 DOUG HARVEY

Harvey was runner-up in 1961–62, the year he left Montreal to join the Rangers as player and head coach and won the Norris Trophy as the league's best defenceman. He stayed in Manhattan two years, retired, then came back to play two games for Detroit in '66–'67 and two more seasons with the Blues in St. Louis.

8 MARCEL DIONNE

Perhaps the greatest player never to win the Stanley Cup, Dionne retired as the third highest points leader in NHL history behind Wayne Gretzky and Gordie Howe. The only time he came close to winning the Hart was 1980, when he was runner-up to Gretzky.

9 GRANT FUHR

Fuhr might be the most underrated goalie of the modern era. He is closing in on his 400th victory and might threaten Terry Sawchuk's all-time record of 447 before his days are done. Fuhr set a record when he played in 79 games in the '95–'96 season with St. Louis. He won five Stanley Cups with the Oilers' dynastic teams of the 1980s.

10 BERNIE PARENT

Although his career was shortened by a serious eye injury, Parent was one of the few skilled players on the Broad Street Bullies' Philadelphia Flyers of the 1970s when the team won back-to-back Stanley Cups in 1974 and '75. In both years, Parent won the Vezina Trophy for phenomenal regular season play as well as the Conn Smythe Trophy for his outstanding goaling in the playoffs. In 1974, he finished second in Hart voting to Phil Esposito of Boston.

Ten Highest **POINT TOTALS** By The Runner-Up In The NHL **SCORING RACE**

1

WAYNE GRETZKY

Los Angeles Kings   1988–89   54 goals 114 assists 168 points

Fellow superstar Mario Lemieux of the Pittsburgh Penguins recorded a personal best 199 points to top The Great One in the 1988–89 scoring race. The high mark of Gretzky's inaugural season in southern California came when he helped the Kings defeat his former team, the Edmonton Oilers, in the first round of the Stanley Cup playoffs.

2

JAROMIR JAGR

Pittsburgh Penguins   1995–96   62 goals 87 assists 149 points

Right-winger Jaromir Jagr was overshadowed by Pittsburgh Penguins teammate Mario Lemieux. The Magnificent One scored 161 points while playing in 70 of his team's 82 games. This represented a triumphant return for Lemieux whose life changed suddenly when he was diagnosed with a form of Hodgkin's disease during the 1992–93 season.

3

WAYNE GRETZKY

Edmonton Oilers   1987–88   40 goals 109 assists 149 points

A 149-point season was sub-par for Gretzky but his total left him trailing only Pittsburgh's budding superstar Mario Lemieux in the scoring race. Gretzky finished the year on a high note by scoring a crucial overtime goal in the Smythe Division finals on the way to the club's fourth Stanley Cup in five seasons.

4

PAT LAFONTAINE

Buffalo Sabres   1992–93   53 goals 95 assists 148 points

A prolific scorer throughout his amateur and professional career, centre Pat Lafontaine was bettered by the Pittsburgh Penguins' incomparable Mario. Lafontaine was placed on the NHL Second All-Star Team ahead of Adam Oates, Doug Gilmour, and Pierre Turgeon, who also enjoyed exceptional seasons.

MIKE BOSSY

5

New York Islanders   1981–82   64 goals 83 assists 147 points

Mike Bossy scored a career high 147 points the year Edmonton's Wayne Gretzky rewrote the NHL record book. He also captured the Conn Smythe Trophy after leading the Islanders to their third consecutive Stanley Cup.

MARIO LEMIEUX

6

Pittsburgh Penguins   1985–86   48 goals 93 assists 141 points

Pittsburgh Penguins' emerging superstar Mario Lemieux scored 141 points in his second NHL season but trailed Wayne Gretzky who amassed an NHL-record 215 points. Lemieux had to wait until 1988–89 to get a taste of post-season action but eventually led the Penguins to consecutive Stanley Cup championships in 1991 and 1992.

BOBBY ORR

7

Boston Bruins   1970–71   37 goals 102 assists 139 points

In a year that saw Boston's Bobby Orr shatter his own single-season scoring record for a defenceman, teammate Phil Esposito established the NHL standard with 76 goals and 152 points. The following year, Orr and Esposito led Boston to its second Stanley Cup in three seasons.

WAYNE GRETZKY

8

Edmonton Oilers   1979–80   51 goals 86 assists 137 points

Edmonton Oilers centre Wayne Gretzky lived up to all expectations during his first NHL season. He tied for the NHL point-scoring lead with Marcel Dionne of Los Angeles but was relegated to second place because he scored fewer goals. Gretzky did capture the Hart Trophy, his first of eight straight. The next season he won the scoring championship to earn his first of seven consecutive Art Ross Trophies.

JARI KURRI

9
Edmonton Oilers   1984–85   71 goals 64 assists 135 points

Edmonton Oilers' sharpshooting right-winger Jari Kurri proved to be the perfect complement to Wayne Gretzky's superlative playmaking. They were never better than the 1984–85 season when Kurri finished second to the Great One in the scoring race. That spring they combined to lead the Oilers to their second consecutive Stanley Cup.

MARCEL DIONNE

10
Los Angeles Kings   1980–81   58 goals 77 assists 135 points

After edging Wayne Gretzky in the previous season's scoring race, Los Angeles Kings centre Marcel Dionne enjoyed a strong 135-point season to finish second in the scoring derby. In the meantime Gretzky exceeded Phil Esposito's single-season point record of 152 by recording 164 points.

GUY CHOUINARD

1 Chouinard formed an effective partnership with Bob MacMillan and Eric Vail on the Atlanta Flames in 1978–79. His 50 goals and 107 points placed him sixth in league scoring that year. A fine skater with natural offensive ability, Chouinard was over-shadowed by other centres of his time. He played in relatively small hockey venues like Atlanta and Calgary. Even when he enjoyed a solid 50-point season as a rookie, Chouinard was surpassed by Calder Trophy-winning teammate Vail.

PAUL MacLEAN

2 A burly right-winger with a handy touch around the net, MacLean scored 41 goals and 101 points for the Winnipeg Jets in 1984–85. He entered the NHL at the mature age of 24 after representing Canada at the 1980 Lake Placid Olympics. MacLean was a tough forward with a good shot who went largely unnoticed by many in the era of Mike Bossy and Jari Kurri.

BOB MacMILLAN

3 MacMillan was a superior playmaking right-winger. In 1978–79, he finished fifth in league scoring with 37 goals and 108 points for the Atlanta Flames. MacMillan played in the shadow of the more celebrated right-wingers of his day, notably Guy Lafleur and Mike Bossy.

DENNIS MARUK

4 A nifty offensive sparkplug, Maruk spent the prime of his career with unsuccessful teams. Toiling admirably for the California Golden Seals, Cleveland Barons, and Washington Capitals, Maruk produced six 30-goal seasons. He followed a 50-goal campaign in 1980–81 with the most unheralded 60-goal output in league history. Maruk's 136-point season was lost in the hoopla surrounding Wayne Gretzky surpassing Phil Esposito's single-season goal-scoring record.

5 JOHN OGRODNICK

A quintessential goal-scorer with a blazing shot, Ogrodnick played his best hockey on a below-average Detroit Red Wings team in the early 1980s. In 1984–85 he won the attention of many in the hockey community with 55 goals and 105 points and placement on the NHL First All-Star team at left wing.

6 BARRY PEDERSON

Pederson was a highly-regarded centre drafted by the Boston Bruins in 1980. He surpassed the 100-point plateau on two occasions during a time when Wayne Gretzky was exceeding 200 points. Injuries — notably the removal of a fibrous tumour from his arm — slowed Pederson's production for the remainder of his career.

7 JEAN PRONOVOST

Pronovost was a consistent right-winger who recorded his only 100-point season for the Pittsburgh Penguins in 1975–76. He played for the most part on a decent team in a relatively small hockey centre. The Penguins were competitive in the regular season but failed to make any significant advances in the post-season.

8 JACQUES RICHARD

Richard demonstrated his immense talent only once in his decade-long NHL career. Unable to speak English, Richard was drafted second overall by the expansion Atlanta Flames in 1972. The culture shock and sudden jump to the NHL curtailed his early development. He later returned to his native Quebec to play with the Nordiques and broke through with 52 goals and 103 points in 1980–81. Richard's accomplishments were overshadowed by the exploits of newly-arrived Peter and Anton Stastny from Czechoslovakia.

MIKE ROGERS

9

Rogers was the least-known player to put together three consecutive 100-point seasons. When the Hartford Whalers joined the league in 1979–80, they had icons Gordie Howe, Dave Keon, and later that year, Bobby Hull in the lineup. Lost in the excitement were Rogers' consecutive 105-point seasons in 1979–80 and 1980–81. Rogers was traded to the New York Rangers where he amassed 103 points.

BLAINE STOUGHTON

10

The NHL's most obscure sharpshooter of the early 1980s, Stoughton began his pro career in the NHL. After enjoying modest success with Pittsburgh and Toronto from 1973 to 1976, he went to the WHA. When he rejoined the NHL, as a member of the Hartford Whalers in 1979–80, he was overshadowed by his famous teammates, Howe, Keon, and Hull, as well as Wayne Gretzky in Edmonton.

Mike Rogers — Hartford

1

WAYNE GRETZKY

31 (10 Art Ross, 9 Hart, 5 Pearson, 5 Lady Byng, 2 Conn Smythe)

Gretzky burst onto the NHL scene with 137 points for the Edmonton Oilers in 1979–80 and won the Hart Trophy and the Lady Byng Trophy. He went on to win a record eight consecutive Harts from 1980 to 1987. In 1980–81 he won his first of seven straight Art Ross Trophies.

2

BOBBY ORR

17 (8 Norris, 3 Hart, 2 Art Ross, 2 Conn Smythe, 1 Pearson, 1 Calder)

The highly-touted prospect made an immediate impact on the Boston Bruins and was presented the Calder Trophy in 1967. He also won the Norris Trophy every year from 1968 to 1975. Orr was presented his first of two Conn Smythe Trophies after he scored the Cup-winning goal in overtime against St. Louis in 1970. He was the first defenceman to lead the NHL in scoring, in 1969–70, a feat he repeated in 1974–75.

3

MARIO LEMIEUX

17 (6 Art Ross, 4 Pearson, 3 Hart, 2 Conn Smythe, 1 Calder, 1 Masterton)

The most anticipated prospect since Wayne Gretzky a few years earlier, Mario Lemieux scored a goal on his first shift and never looked back. He won the Calder Trophy in 1985 and within a few years won three Hart Trophies. Lemieux won the Lester B. Pearson Trophy and was presented the Masterton Award in 1993 after his successful battle against a form of Hodgkin's disease.

4

GORDIE HOWE

12 (6 Hart, 6 Art Ross)

Howe played during five decades in the NHL but his most successful period was with the Detroit Red Wings in 1950s and 1960s. He won five of his six Art Ross Trophies between 1951 and 1957 and was awarded the Hart Trophy six times between 1952 and 1963. "Mr. Hockey" was considered the complete player who was as tough as he was skilled.

Different **FORMATS** Of The **NHL** **ALL-STAR** Game

1

BENEFIT GAMES

Ace Bailey Benefit Game — February 14, 1934

Howie Morenz Memorial Game — November 3, 1937

Babe Siebert Memorial Game — October 29, 1939

The present-day NHL All-Star Weekend originated with three charity games played in the 1930s. The first took place at Maple Leaf Gardens to raise money for Toronto forward Ace Bailey, whose career had ended abruptly two months earlier. The hometown Maple Leafs triumphed 7–3.

Four years later the hockey world mourned the untimely death of Canadiens' superstar Howie Morenz. A memorial game to aid his family was held at the Montreal Forum early in the 1937–38 season. The NHL All-Stars skated against players from both Montreal clubs, the Canadiens *and* Maroons, and won 6–5.

Following the tragic off-season drowning of Habs' star Albert "Babe" Siebert, the third benefit game of the decade was set for the Montreal Forum on the eve of the 1939–40 schedule. Toronto centre Syl Apps recorded four points to lead the NHL All-Stars to a 5–2 win over the Montreal Canadiens.

2

STARS VS. CUP CHAMPIONS

1947–48 to 1950–51, 1953–54 to 1967–68

Some of the fiercest All-Star games pitted the Stanley Cup holders against the best the NHL had to offer. One of the top games was the inaugural contest at Maple Leaf Gardens on October 13, 1947. Toronto held a 3–1 advantage but yielded goals to Grant Warwick, Maurice Richard, and Doug Bentley to lose 4–3.

3

FIRST ALL-STARS VS. SECOND ALL-STARS

1951–52 & 1952–53

The First and Second All-Star teams from the previous season squared off in Toronto on October 9, 1951. The First All-Star team was enhanced by players chosen from the U.S. clubs, while the Second All-Star Team was buoyed by performers from the two Canadian franchises. The following season the Detroit Olympia played host to a 1–1 tie. This was the lowest scoring All-Star Game in the history of the event.

EAST VS. WEST
1968–69 to 1973–74

The NHL doubled in size following the first major expansion in 1967, and in 1968 the All-Star game was a battle between the two divisions. Over the six years of this format the East enjoyed a 3–2–1 advantage over the West. Bobby Hull earned the unique distinction of winning consecutive game MVP awards in 1970 and 1971. The former was earned as a member of the East team while the latter came as a member of the West squad after the Chicago Blackhawks switched divisions in the off-season.

WALES VS. CAMPBELL
1974–75 to 1992–93

The Wales Conference All-Stars charged ahead with five straight wins from 1975 to 1980. The Campbell Conference gained revenge in 1983 when Wayne Gretzky scored four times in the third period to lead the squad to a 9–3 victory. On January 21, 1990, the inaugural NHL All-Star Weekend added a skills competition and Heroes of Hockey exhibition game to the festivities. The Wales Conference won 12 of the 17 games played.

EASTERN VS. WESTERN
1993–94 to 1996–97*

The further expansion of the game into the United States caused a change in name: the conferences were retitled as the more simple Eastern and Western. The Eastern (Wales) Conference continued its mastery with three straight wins over the Western (Campbell) Conference.

*The 1994–95 NHL All-Star Game was cancelled as a result of the owners' lockout

A more competitive format was introduced for the 1998 All-Star Game in Vancouver inspired by the participation of the NHL's top stars at the upcoming Olympics in Nagano, Japan. The influx of European players into the NHL since the early 1980s had caused a schism among fans and players. In the initial confrontation, North America topped the World 8–7. Some critics suggested that the format excluded too many worthy players from the deeper North American pool.

Ten **LOWEST CAREER GOALS**-Against
Averages At The **ALL-STAR GAME**
(minimum two games played)

1

GILLES VILLEMURE 0.68

Villemure allowed just one goal in 1973, to go with shutouts in his half of the two previous games, 1972 and 1971. He represented the Rangers in all three appearances and had a record of 1–0–0.

2

GERRY McNEIL 1.49

McNeil played three successive games — 1951, 1952, and 1953 — all as a member of the Habs. He gave up just three goals in 120 total minutes played, though he never won a game (0–1–2).

3

JOHNNY BOWER 1.50

Bower played in four All-Star games, three as a member of the Stanley Cup champion Toronto Maple Leafs. He allowed just four goals in more than 159 minutes played, and had a 2–0–0 record.

4

FRANK BRIMSEK 1.51

Brimsek played in three games, including the Babe Siebert Memorial game, and won each while allowing just three goals along the way.

5

GUMP WORSLEY 1.63

The Gumper played four games with three teams, '61 and '62 for the Rangers, '65 for the Habs, and '72 for the North Stars. In 110 minutes played, he let in only three goals but had three no-decisions to go with a loss in 1972.

6

DON EDWARDS 2.03

Edwards played twice at the All-Star game, 1980 and 1982, allowing two goals the first time and none the second. He represented Buffalo on both occasions, and had a 1–0 record.

7   KEN DRYDEN   2.40

In five All-Star appearances, Dryden allowed five goals and shut out the opposition for his half of the 1975 game. He played the 1972 game as a rookie, and his All-Star career had five no-decisions.

8   GLENN HALL   2.44

The incredible Hall played 13 All-Star games and 540 minutes, more than any other goalie. Three times he shut out the other team. He allowed 22 goals and had a 4–4 record with five no-decisions. His first game was in 1955 and his last in 1969. He represented three teams — Detroit, Chicago, and St. Louis.

9   TERRY SAWCHUK   2.44

Sawchuk's eleven appearances are second only to Hall, but he bested Hall in teams represented. Sawchuk played 1950–54 and 1959 and 1963 as a member of Detroit, '55 and '56 for Boston, 1964 for Toronto, and '68 for the L.A. Kings.

10   CHARLIE RAYNER   2.63

Rayner played three times in a row (1949–51), all for the Rangers games he played. The wandering goalie let in four goals in the three half-games he played.

Alex Connell

1

CLINT BENEDICT

The first year the Vezina was awarded, at the end of the 1926–27 season, Benedict was the runner-up, despite recording 13 shutouts in 43 games to go with a 1.42 GAA. George Hainsworth had one more shut-out and won 28 games. Benedict was never again even runner-up. For "Praying Benny," his most dominant years were those just before the introduction of the trophy, when he led the league in wins for six successive seasons.

2

DAN BOUCHARD

Bouchard was never a runner-up for the Vezina, though he played for 14 years and won 286 games. His best season was '78–'79, when he won 32 games, but he never had more than five shutouts in a year, and he played for mostly mediocre teams — the Atlanta Flames, Quebec Nordiques, and Winnipeg Jets.

3

GERRY CHEEVERS

Cheesie's career spanned three decades and two Cups with the Bruins, but the closest he ever came to the goalie hardware was in his last season, when he was runner-up. Although a flamboyant goalie, he played during the prime of perennial Vezina winners Tony Esposito, Bernie Parent, and Ken Dryden.

4

ALEX CONNELL

Three times Connell was second in Vezina voting, but never first. He was runner-up to George Hainsworth in 1928, Charlie Gardiner in 1932, and Lorne Chabot in '35. Despite recording 81 career shutouts, a 1.91 career average, and playing eight full seasons without missing a game, he never won the trophy during his Hall of Fame career.

5

ROGER CROZIER

Crozier won both the Calder and Conn Smythe Trophies, but never the Vezina. His first year was by far his best. In '64–'65, he won an incredible 40 games, but then had seasons of 27, 22, and 9 wins. He never won even 25 games in another year, despite playing for Buffalo in the franchise's successful early years, when they made it to the finals in 1975.

6

ED GIACOMIN

Twice a runner-up for the Vezina, Giacomin was an out-standing goalie with the Rangers for more than a decade. He won 30 games five times and helped the Broadway Blueshirts get to the finals in 1972. (The team lost to Bobby Orr's Bruins.) He was elected to the Hockey Hall of Fame in 1987.

7

MIKE LIUT

Liut was runner-up in 1987 to Ron Hextall for the Vezina, but despite winning 294 career games never won the trophy, in large measure because he played with unsuccessful teams (St. Louis, Hartford, and Washington).

8

ANDY MOOG

Moog was never even a runner-up for the Vezina, despite winning 20 games eleven times, and three Stanley Cups with the Oilers' dynasty of the early 1980s. He played in four All-Star games, represented Canada at the 1988 Olympics in Calgary, and finished his career in Montreal in 1997–98.

9

MIKE VERNON

One-time runner-up to Patrick Roy in 1989, Vernon is still going strong and adding to his 350-plus victories. He was instrumental in Calgary winning the 1989 Stanley Cup, and after 12 years with the Flames he led the Wings to a 1996 Cup victory, when he won the Conn Smythe. He joined the San Jose Sharks that summer.

Eight **GOALTENDERS** To Play For **BOTH** The Toronto Maple **LEAFS** And Montreal **CANADIENS**

1 GEORGE HAINSWORTH

Between 1926 and 1929, George Hainsworth won three consecutive Vezina Trophies in the Montreal net. In 1928–29, he established an NHL single-season record with 22 shutouts. He played three seasons in Toronto where he helped the Leafs finish in first place on two occasions. Hainsworth was elected to the Hockey Hall of Fame in 1961.

2 LORNE CHABOT

Montreal native "Sad Eyes" Chabot spent half his NHL career with Toronto. Chabot's strong effort enabled the team to win its first Stanley Cup as the Maple Leafs in 1931–32. Before the 1933–34 season, he was sent to the Canadiens for George Hainsworth, making them the first two goalies to play for both clubs.

3 PAUL BIBEAULT

Beginning in 1940–41 Paul Bibeault played parts of four seasons with the Canadiens, and was signed by the Maple Leafs following his discharge from the Canadian Army. Bibeault's play earned him selection to the NHL Second All-Star team. He was the son-in-law of legendary general manager Frank Selke, Sr.

4 JACQUES PLANTE

Plante's accomplishments included backstopping the Canadiens to a league-record five consecutive Stanley Cups from 1955–56 to 1959–60 and pioneering the use of a goal mask beginning on November 1, 1959. He played for the New York Rangers, then the St. Louis Blues, and joined Toronto before the 1970–71 season and later tutored emerging star Bernie Parent. He was elected to the Hockey Hall of Fame in 1978.

5 CESARE MANIAGO

Although best remembered from his days with the Minnesota North Stars from 1967–68 to 1975–76, Maniago began his NHL tenure by playing seven games for Toronto in 1960–61. He took part in fourteen games with the Habs in his sophomore season. Maniago appeared briefly with the Rangers before heading to the expansion North Stars where he formed a strong netminding partnership with Gump Worsley.

6 MICHEL LAROCQUE

"Bunny" Larocque joined the Montreal Canadiens when they were shaping an already strong club into a Stanley Cup dynasty. He won four straight Stanley Cups from 1976 to 1979 and shared the Vezina Trophy with his partner Ken Dryden in each of those seasons. Late in the 1980–81 season he was acquired by the Leafs.

7 WAYNE THOMAS

Early in his career in Montreal, Wayne Thomas had trouble earning steady playing time due to the presence of Ken Dryden. When Dryden spent the 1974–75 campaign pursuing legal studies, Thomas got into 42 contests. Dryden resumed his NHL career the following year forcing Thomas back to the minors. His fortunes took a positive turn in 1975 when the Toronto Maple Leafs traded for his services. Thomas enjoyed his best season in 1975–76 when he recorded 28 wins and was chosen to play in the NHL All-Star game.

8 RICK WALMSLEY

Walmsley spent parts of four seasons with the Montreal Canadiens in the early 1980s. He moved on to St. Louis and Calgary, where he won a Stanley Cup in 1989. He joined Toronto following a trade in 1992.

Ten Famous Goalies' FIRST SHUTOUTS

1

TERRY SAWCHUK
January 15, 1950 Detroit 1 Rangers 0

Sawchuk was called up for seven games during the '49–'50
season from the farm in Indianapolis. During that stretch he
recorded his first of a record 103 career regular-season shutouts
(to go with 12 more in the playoffs). The next year he became the
Wings' number one goalie, and in the next six years missed only
14 games with Detroit.

2

JOHNNY BOWER
January 14, 1954 Rangers 2 Chicago 0

After nine years in the minors, Bower played every game for the
Rangers in 1953–54, then spent most of the next four years in the
minors again before being rescued by Toronto. This was his first of
37 shutouts to complement four Stanley Cups with the Leafs.

3

GLENN HALL
January 8, 1953 Detroit 4 Boston 0

Hall played his first six NHL games mid-season as a call-up in
'52–'53 after an injury sidelined Sawchuk. After the Wings traded
Sawchuk, Hall became Detroit's main man in goal for the next two
years before establishing himself in Chicago and finishing his career
in St. Louis. He finished with 84 lifetime shutouts.

4

JACQUES PLANTE
February 20, 1954 Canadiens 2 Detroit 0

Plante played the final 17 games of the '53–'54 season while netminding incumbent Gerry McNeil recovered from an injury. In those
17 games, Plante recorded an amazing five shutouts and became
the starting goalie the next fall. He won five successive Vezina
Trophies (1956–60), added another in 1962, and shared a seventh
with Glenn Hall in St. Louis in 1969.

KEN DRYDEN

October 22, 1971   Canadiens 6   Vancouver 0

Dryden had all eight of Montreal's shutouts in the 1971–72 season and won the Calder Trophy *after* leading the team to a Stanley Cup in the spring of 1971, when he was also awarded the Conn Smythe. He played just 397 games in the NHL but had 46 shutouts and won the Cup six times.

GRANT FUHR

December 30, 1983   Edmonton 2   Boston 0

Arguably the best goalie of the 1980s, Fuhr did not get his first shutout behind the most dangerous offence in NHL history until his third full season in the league. His 23 career shutouts seem small compared to other greats, but in an era of offence Fuhr's Oiler teammates routinely credited him for much of their Stanley Cup success.

Grant Fuhr

7 DOMINIK HASEK
January 16, 1992   Chicago 4   Toronto 0

Hasek was nearly 27 years old before he got his first shutout,
midway through his second partial season with his first NHL team,
the Chicago Blackhawks. He was traded that summer to Buffalo
for Stephane Beauregard and a fourth-round draft choice in 1993
(Eric Daze) and now has more than 40 career shutouts.

8 CURTIS JOSEPH
December 19, 1991   St. Louis 4   San Jose 0

"CUJO" didn't get his first shutout until his third season in the
league. He now has more than 20, and another seven in the playoffs, and has won more than 250 games with the three teams he's
played for — St. Louis, Edmonton, and Toronto.

9 PATRICK ROY
January 15, 1986   Canadiens 4   Winnipeg 0

Roy became a hero his first full year with the Canadiens, winning
the Conn Smythe Trophy as a rookie and leading the Habs to an
improbable Stanley Cup. Although he is not known as a shutout
goaltender, he is one of only four men to win 400 games and is
closing in on Terry Sawchuk's record of 447.

10 FRANK BRIMSEK
December 4, 1938   Boston 5   Chicago 0

"Mister Zero" earned his nickname for wearing "0" at the All-Star
game, but he also had 40 career shutouts in ten years in the NHL,
including ten in his rookie season, 1938–39, in which he won the
Calder Trophy. He was particularly durable, missing just 20 games
during his 514-game career.

Eight Best **GOALIES** To Play **U.S. COLLEGE** Or **HIGH SCHOOL** Hockey

1 KEN DRYDEN

The Boston Bruins selected Ken Dryden at the 1964
Amateur Draft, then promptly dealt him to the Montreal Canadiens.
He played for Cornell University before suiting up for Canada at the
1969 World Championships and spending a year with the National
Team. Late in the 1970–71 campaign Dryden went undefeated in
six regular season games then led the Habs to a surprise Stanley
Cup win. His heroics earned him the Conn Smythe Trophy.

2 TONY ESPOSITO

Esposito starred at Michigan Tech from 1964 to 1967. In
June, 1969, he was claimed by Chicago in the Intra-League Draft
and went on to record 15 shutouts in 1969–70 and win the Calder
and Vezina trophies. "Tony O" retired in 1984 with 76 shutouts and
423 wins in 886 regular season appearances.

3 ED BELFOUR

After playing a year with the University of North Dakota
in 1986–87, Belfour was signed as a free agent by the Chicago
Blackhawks. He took the NHL by storm by winning a league-high
43 games and helping the Hawks finish at the top of the regular
season standings. He was presented the Calder, Vezina, and
Jennings trophies. In 1998–99 he backstopped the Dallas Stars to
the Stanley Cup.

4 TOM BARRASSO

The Buffalo Sabres chose Barrasso fifth overall in the
1983 Entry Draft out of Acton-Boxboro High School. This was the
earliest an American goalie had ever been drafted. Barrasso lived up
to his advance billing and won the Calder and Vezina trophies in
1984. In 1988–89 he was traded to Pittsburgh where he contributed
to Stanley Cup wins in 1991 and 1992.

5 CURTIS JOSEPH

Originally signed as a free agent by St. Louis in June, 1989, Joseph starred for the University of Wisconsin in 1988–89. Beginning in 1989–90 he played five seasons with the Blues, where he recorded 137 regular season wins. "Cujo" was then shipped to Edmonton where he helped the team reach the second round of the Stanley Cup playoffs in 1997 and 1998. In July, 1998, he signed as a free agent with the Toronto Maple Leafs.

6 MIKE RICHTER

Before joining the NHL, Mike Richter starred with the University of Wisconsin and represented the U.S. at the 1985 and 1986 World Junior Championships, the 1986 and 1987 World Championships, and the 1988 Calgary Olympics. His netminding heroics were a key factor in the Rangers' first Stanley Cup in 50 years in 1994. In 1996 Richter led the USA to victory in the inaugural World Cup of Hockey and he was selected tournament MVP.

7 GLENN RESCH

Resch spent four years at the University of Minnesota-Duluth from 1967 to 1971. Before their NHL debut in 1972, the New York Islanders acquired his services from Montreal. Between 1973–74 and 1980–81 he won 154 regular season games for the Isles before being traded to New Jersey.

8 JON CASEY

Casey excelled at the University of North Dakota, where he was chosen the WCHA First All-Star team goalie in 1982 and 1984. He played for the U.S. at the 1982 World Junior championships and was signed as a free agent by the Minnesota North Stars in April, 1984. His best NHL season was 1989–90 when he recorded an NHL-leading 31 wins.

Ten Best GOALIES Who CAUGHT RIGHT

1

TOM BARRASSO

Despite missing most of 1994–95 and 1996–97 with serious shoulder injuries, Barrasso has more than 350 career wins, including 43 in 1992–93. He has played with the Penguins since early in the '88–'89 season, after being traded by Buffalo with a draft pick for Doug Bodger and Darrin Shannon.

2

CLINT BENEDICT

The man who wore a face mask briefly after sustaining a face injury in 1928, Benedict played five years with the Ottawa Senators in the National Hockey Association before the team joined the NHL in 1917. In 1924 he joined the Montreal Maroons for six seasons, and during his 13 years in the NHL he led the league in wins nine times, shutouts seven times, and average six times.

3

ALEX CONNELL

Connell inherited Benedict's mantle as goaler in Ottawa and was the league's iron man, playing every game for his first six years. In 12 years he recorded 81 shutouts and was key to the team's 1927 Stanley Cup victory.

4

ROGER CROZIER

Crozier was one of a few goalies to win the Calder Trophy (in 1965), and the next year won the Conn Smythe for his brilliant performance in the '66 playoffs, which his Wings lost to the Canadiens in six games. He joined the expansion Buffalo Sabres in 1970 and for six years helped build the team into a contender. In 1976–77, he made three appearances with the lowly Washington Capitals before he retired.

5 BILL DURNAN

The only ambidextrous goalie in league history, he played with the Canadiens for only seven years (1943–50). Durnan was the last goaler to be a team captain and won the Stanley Cup twice with the *bleu, blanc, et rouge*. He was inducted into the Hockey Hall of Fame in 1964.

6 TONY ESPOSITO

Although he played 13 games with Montreal in 1968–69, Esposito was a Chicago Blackhawk through and through for some 15 years. His 423 career wins places him second all time behind only the great Terry Sawchuk, and his 76 shutouts are also a post-Sawchuk record not likely to be matched for decades. Perhaps the only blight on his otherwise illustrious career was that he never won a Stanley Cup.

7 GRANT FUHR

Because he played the formative years of his career with an offensively explosive Edmonton Oilers team, Fuhr is one of the great overlooked goalies. But after almost 20 years and 400 wins, his career achievements will forever remain true testaments to his greatness. He won five Stanley Cups with the Oilers, won 20 games in a season eleven times, and holds records for most games (79) and minutes played (4,365) in a single season.

8 GEORGE HAINSWORTH

Hainsworth was another iron man, missing only two games in ten years from 1926–36 with the Canadiens and Toronto. In eleven seasons, he recorded an incredible 94 shutouts, including a record 22 in '28–'29, a 44–game season. His career goals against average is 1.91, and his short NHL career was preceded by more than 15 years in senior hockey and the minor pro leagues.

9 DAVE KERR

Kerr led the Rangers to a Stanley Cup in 1939–40 and for five years started every game for the Broadway Blueshirts. He began his NHL life with the Montreal Maroons and cross-town New York rivals, the Americans. He had a win percentage of better than .600 and 51 career shutouts.

10   TINY THOMPSON

Thompson was a true superstar with the Bruins for much of the 1920s and '30s thanks largely to his first-year success in which the Bruins won the Cup. For ten years, he started every game but one, and in '29–'30 had an incredible record of 38–5–1. He averaged almost 24 wins a season (in a 48–game schedule) for a dozen years. He was traded early in '38–'39 to Detroit, the same season Boston won the hardware again.

Dave Kerr

FIRST TEN Goalies To Play For The Los Angeles KINGS

1 ### WAYNE RUTLEDGE

On October 14, 1967, Rutledge backstopped the L.A. Kings to a 4–2 win in their NHL debut. Later that season he recorded the first Kings shutout, versus the St. Louis Blues. The 1967–68 season represented the high point of Rutledge's NHL tenure when he recorded 20 wins.

2 ### TERRY SAWCHUK

In the 1967 NHL expansion draft the Kings were fortunate to obtain Terry Sawchuk from the Stanley Cup champion Toronto Maple Leafs. He completed the 1967–68 season with two shutouts and a 3.07 goals against average. Sawchuk played two more seasons, one with the Red Wings and one with Rangers, before retiring as the NHL's all-time shutout leader with 103.

Terry Sawchuk in the L.A. net

JACQUES CARON

3

Jacques Caron was in the midst of his sixth year as a minor pro goalie when he was called up to play one game for the L.A. Kings against the St. Louis Blues on December 27, 1967. In 1971–72 he made 28 appearances for St. Louis, registering a shutout and 14 victories. The following season Caron made 30 appearances but could not hold a steady position after that.

GERRY DESJARDINS

4

The Kings acquired Gerry Desjardins from the Montreal Canadiens' organization prior to the 1968–69 season. After stops in three more NHL cities and the WHA, Desjardins retired with NHL totals of 12 shutouts and 122 regular season wins along with a 3.29 career goals against average.

DENIS DEJORDY

5

The Kings received Dejordy as part of the package obtained from Chicago in return for Gerry Desjardins and defence-man Bill White in 1969–70. Dejordy spent parts of three seasons with Los Angeles before moving on briefly to Montreal and Detroit. He retired following 1973–74 with 15 shutouts and 124 regular season wins.

JACK NORRIS

6

Norris played the last 25 games of his NHL career as Denis Dejordy's backup in 1970–71. His career was rejuvenated with the formation of the World Hockey Association. Between 1972–73 and 1975–76 he played 191 regular season games for the Alberta/Edmonton Oilers and the Phoenix Roadrunners. Norris led all WHA netminders by appearing in 64 regular season games for Alberta in 1972–73.

7 GARY EDWARDS

The Kings acquired Edwards from Buffalo in the Intra-League Draft in June, 1971. He played 44 games as an L.A. rookie in 1971–72 and played 101 games over the next four seasons while earning the reputation as one of the league's most dependable backup netminders. Edwards played in Cleveland, Minnesota, Edmonton, St. Louis, and Pittsburgh before retiring with 88 regular season wins and 11 shutouts.

8 ROGATIEN VACHON

Los Angeles acquired Vachon from the Montreal Canadiens in November, 1971. He remained with the Kings through the 1977–78 schedule when he left as one of the most popular and successful players in team history. In 1976 he backstopped Canada to the inaugural Canada Cup championship and was placed on the tournament all-star team. He retired with regular season totals of 51 shutouts, 355 victories, and a 2.99 goals against mark.

9 BILLY SMITH

Smith began his career with a five-game stint for the L.A. Kings in 1971–72. He was chosen by the New York Islanders in the 1972 Expansion Draft and later backstopped the team to four consecutive Stanley Cups between 1979–80 and 1982–83. He retired with 22 shutouts and 305 wins. Smith was the winner of the Vezina Trophy in 1982 and the Conn Smythe Trophy in 1983. He was elected to the Hockey Hall of Fame in 1993.

10 GARY SIMMONS

Simmons made his last 19 NHL regular season and playoff appearances as member of the L.A. Kings. He enjoyed his most successful years with the California Golden Seals in 1974–75 and 1975–76, when he won 25 games in 74 contests. He retired in 1977–78 after registering five shutouts and a career goals against average of 3.56.

Most **PENALTY SHOTS** Faced By
A Goalie

Kelly Hrudey is one of only two goalies (the other is Glenn Hall) to face 12 penalty shots in his career. He stopped six.

1   January 26, 1984, **scored** on by Michel Goulet (Quebec) in 5–1 New York loss.

2   October 13, 1984, **scored** on by Bill Gardner (Chicago) in 7–6 New York win.

3   November 18, 1984, **stopped** Ron Sutter (Philadelphia) in 3–3 New York tie.

4   December 2, 1986, **scored** on by Joe Mullen (Calgary) in 3–3 New York tie.

5   January 19, 1988, **scored** on by Mario Lemieux (Pittsburgh) in 6–4 New York loss.

6   March 7, 1989, **scored** on by Mario Lemieux (Pittsburgh) in 3–2 Los Angeles win.

7   February 5, 1991, **scored** on by Norm Lacombe (Philadelphia) in 3–2 Los Angeles win.

8   February 2, 1993, **stopped** Mats Sundin (Quebec) in 3–2 Los Angeles loss.

9   October 6, 1993, **stopped** Pavel Bure (Vancouver) in 5–2 Los Angeles loss.

10   January 27, 1994, **stopped** Tony Amonte (Rangers) in 5–4 Los Angeles loss.

11   February 12, 1995, **stopped** Sergei Fedorov (Detroit) in 4–4 Los Angeles tie.

12   March 9, 1995, **stopped** Dirk Graham (Chicago) in 4–3 Los Angeles win.

Most **PENALTY SHOTS** Taken By
One Player

Mario Lemieux holds all-time NHL records both for most penalty shots taken — eight — and penalty shots scored — six.

1 December 29, 1984, **beat** Mario Gosselin in a 10–2 loss to the Nordiques.

2 January 19, 1988, **beat** Kelly Hrudey in a 6–4 win over the Islanders.

3 December 31, 1988, **beat** Chris Terreri in an 8–6 win over the Devils.

4 March 7, 1989, **beat** Kelly Hrudey in a 3–2 loss to Los Angeles.

5 November 24, 1989, **beat** Bob Mason in a 7–4 win over Washington.

6 March 17, 1992, **stopped** by Bill Ranford in a 6–5 win over Edmonton.

7 March 23, 1996, **stopped** by Dominik Hasek in a 7–5 loss to Buffalo.

8 April 11, 1997, **beat** John Vanbiesbrouck in a 4–2 loss to Florida.

Ten **UNDRAFTED GOALIES** Who Played In The **NHL**

1

ED BELFOUR

Belfour had an incredible year at University of North Dakota in 1986–87, going 29–4 before being signed that fall by Chicago at the age of 22. By the end of his rookie season, he had won an unprecedented three major trophies, the Calder, Vezina, and Jennings. He has gone on to play more than 500 games in the NHL — winning more than half — in a career that is now in its thirteenth year and that culminated in a 1999 Stanley Cup season.

2

JON CASEY

For four years, no one gave Jon Casey a good look. He, too, attended the U of North Dakota, from 1980 to 1984, and was signed as a free agent by Minnesota almost immediately after graduating. He played more than 23,000 minutes in the NHL with three teams (the North Stars, Boston, and St. Louis), and represented the United States at both the World Junior Championships and World Championships.

3

ALAIN CHEVRIER

Chevrier played at the little-scouted University of Miami-Ohio for four years and played a full season in the IHL after that before any team took a chance on him. He wound up playing for five teams in his six-year career, with a record of 91–100–14 and two shutouts.

4

MICHEL DION

Dion did not join the NHL until he was nearly 26 years old. After playing with the Montreal Junior Canadiens, he played in the WHA for five seasons before being claimed by Quebec when the Nordiques entered the league in 1979. He played six years in the NHL, and in 1981–82 had a record of 25–24–12 in Pittsburgh.

5   BRIAN HAYWARD

After four years at Cornell where he went unnoticed by scouts, Hayward joined the Winnipeg Jets for 1981–82 and went 24–10–12 in his rookie year. In eleven NHL seasons, he won 20 games three times, including 33 in '84–'85 with the Jets, and for three consecutive years won the Jennings Trophy with Patrick Roy in Montreal.

6   GLENN HEALY

Another goalie to play for an American university — Western Michigan — Healy signed with Los Angeles and started a 13-year career that continues to this day. He has played in more than 400 games and is one of only a few players to play for both New York teams in consecutive seasons, the Islanders in '92–'93 and the Rangers in '93–'94.

7   CURTIS JOSEPH

"CUJO" was free for the asking in 1989 when the Blues signed him to a contract, and for four successive seasons improved the team by winning 16, 27, 29, and 36 games. In his last three seasons, two with Edmonton and one with Toronto, he almost became the third goalie in NHL history, after Glenn Hall and Sugar Jim Henry, to play 70 games in each year (he played 67 with Toronto in 1998–99).

8   CHICO RESCH

Resch's four strong years with the University of Minnesota-Duluth got him as far as the IHL. Two years later the Islanders signed him as back-up to Billy Smith, and he won the first two of four Cups the Long Islanders won in the early 1980s. He played with the Rockies, New Jersey, and Philadelphia before retiring after 571 games and more than 32,000 NHL minutes played.

9 ROBERTO ROMANO

Romano didn't impress scouts as a teenager despite excelling in the QMJHL for four years. He spent a year in the minors before the Penguins signed him in 1982 for nothing, but he never became a regular. In six NHL seasons, he played 3, 18, 31, 46, 26, and 2 games, and spent most of his career in Italy before retiring after the '93–'94 season.

10 WAYNE THOMAS

Thomas was 25 before he played in the NHL and was one of only eight goalies to play for both Toronto and Montreal. He also played for the Rangers during his 243-game career. He was Toronto property before he ever played for the team, but the Leafs traded him to Los Angeles and the Kings to Montreal. In the summer of 1975, after two years with the Habs, he was traded back to Toronto.

Curtis Joseph

1 PITTSBURGH PENGUINS 1984

Mario Lemieux 1st, Doug Bodger 9th, Roger Belanger 16th

The Penguins were fortunate to finish last in the NHL's standings in 1983–84. They selected Laval Titan junior phenom Mario Lemieux with the first overall pick. He spent his entire career with Pittsburgh where he led the club to consecutive Stanley Cups in 1991 and 1992. He also led the NHL in scoring on six occasions and was a three-time winner of the Hart Trophy. Bodger was a strong offensive blueliner who was the key figure in the package the Pens sent to Buffalo to acquire goalie Tom Barrasso in 1988–89. Belanger only played one NHL season but the performances of the other two picks made this a bountiful year for Pittsburgh.

2 TORONTO MAPLE LEAFS 1973

Lanny McDonald 4th, Bob Neely 10th, Ian Turnbull 15th

After a poor season in 1972–73 the Toronto Maple Leafs became a solid club again — until 1978–79. Their upswing was influenced by McDonald and Turnbull becoming two of the NHL's best at their respective positions. McDonald was Darryl Sittler's right-winger and registered three straight 40-goal seasons for the Leafs. Turnbull topped the 60-point mark four times and became the first defence-man to score five goals in a game. Neely spent four seasons in Toronto where he supplied muscle from his left-wing position and posted 89 points in 261 regular season games.

3 MONTREAL CANADIENS 1974

Cam Connor 5th, Doug Risebrough 7th, Rick Chartraw 10th,
Mario Tremblay 12th

Doug Risebrough and Mario Tremblay formed two-thirds of one of the Habs' key forward lines on their four straight Stanley Cups from 1976 to 1979. Tremblay was also part of Montreal's championship in 1986. Chartraw was a solid defencemen who logged a great deal of ice time on the 1970s dynasty. Connor turned out to be the disappointment of the group but did score a famous goal in double overtime against the Toronto Maple Leafs in the 1979 quarterfinals.

BOSTON BRUINS 1970

Reggie Leach 3rd, Rick MacLeish 4th, Ron Plumb 9th, Bob Stewart 13th

The Bruins chose well with their first two picks in 1970 but the potential of these choices came to fruition in Philadelphia. Leach was sent to California in 1971–72 and became one of the league's top scorers from 1974 to 1982. MacLeish was a key player on the Flyers' Cup wins in 1974 and 1975. Ironically, he scored the Cup winner against Boston in game six of the 1974 Final. Plumb was lured to the WHA and only played one NHL season. Stewart played 575 games for three teams.

PHILADELPHIA FLYERS 1978

Behn Wilson 6th, Ken Linseman 7th, Danny Lucas 14th

The Flyers selected two of the best players to come out of the draft, Behn Wilson and Ken Linseman. Wilson provided offence and toughness on the Philly blueline and helped the team reach the 1980 Stanley Cup Final. Linseman was a tenacious two-way centre and spent parts of four seasons with the Flyers before he was sent to Hartford. Lucas played only six NHL games but this was still a highly successful year for the Flyers' franchise.

BUFFALO SABRES 1982

Phil Housley 6th, Paul Cyr 9th, Dave Andreychuk 16th

The Buffalo Sabres retooled in the early 1980s under the guidance of coach and general manager Scotty Bowman. Phil Housley was a slick offensive defencemen who reached the 20-goal mark five times for Buffalo. Cyr scored 84 goals for the Sabres from 1982 to 1987 before he was traded to the Rangers. Andreychuk was the best pick of the three, with seven 30-goal seasons to his credit in Buffalo.

BUFFALO SABRES 1983

Tom Barrasso 5th, Normand Lacombe 10th, Adam Creighton 11th

Barrasso won 26 games in 1983–84 and was chosen the Calder and Vezina Trophy winner. He was eventually traded to Pittsburgh and helped the Penguins win consecutive Stanley Cups in 1991 and 1992. Lacombe played 94 games for the Sabres. Creighton never lived up to expectations in Buffalo but scored 34 goals for Chicago in 1990–91. In the trade with the Hawks, the Sabres obtained Rick Vaive who scored 29 goals in 1989–90 and 25 the following year.

TEN BEST Players DRAFTED From The
OTTAWA 67's

1 BILL CLEMENT

Clement was drafted eighteenth overall by Philadelphia in 1970 and joined the Flyers after one year in the AHL with the Quebec Aces. He played a dozen years in the NHL, winning two Cups with the "Broad Street Bullies" in '74 and '75 and playing in two All-Star games (1976 and 1978).

2 ADAM CREIGHTON

Creighton never quite lived up to the potential he was thought to have when Buffalo drafted him eleventh overall in 1983. It took him seven years to play a full season (with Chicago), and he never became the scoring threat his one 30-goal season suggested. In 708 career games, he scored 187 times with five different teams.

3 RANDY CUNNEYWORTH

A fairy-tale story, Cunneyworth made it to the NHL despite being drafted an improbable 167th overall. He played most of four seasons with the Rochester Americans of the AHL before the Penguins finally gave him a big-league chance in 1985. Cunneyworth went on to captain the Senators, and was called up by the Sabres in last year's Stanley Cup finals.

4 PETER LEE

Lee played nearly five full seasons with the 67's, and although he was drafted by Montreal in 1976, he was traded to Pittsburgh with Pete Mahovlich for Pierre Larouche and future considerations (Peter Marsh). A couple of years later, Larouche scored 50 goals for the Habs. Although Lee twice scored 30, his stock never rose very high. After six years in Pittsburgh, Lee went to Germany where he played for eight years with Dusseldorfer EG.

STEVE PAYNE

5

Payne was Minnesota's second selection at the 1978 draft, nineteenth overall, and joined the Stars after two seasons of junior. He played his entire ten-year, 613-game career with the North Stars. He had four consecutive 30-goal seasons, but in '87–'88 played only nine games before ending up in the IHL with Kalamazoo.

DENIS POTVIN

6

Potvin played five years of junior with the 67's (1968–73) before being drafted first overall in 1973 by the Islanders. He played all of his 1,060 NHL games on Long Island, winning four Stanley Cups with the team and scoring 20 goals in a season nine times. He won the Norris Trophy three times and was the first defenceman to reach the 1,000-point mark. He was inducted into the Hockey Hall of Fame in 1991.

GARY ROBERTS

7

A phenomenal power forward in his heyday, Roberts spent the majority of his career with Calgary before retiring due to serious neck injuries. After a year of rest, however, he felt well enough to come back and joined Carolina, where he scored 20 goals his first year. A former 50-goal scorer, Roberts has had 200 penalty minutes five times during his career.

BOBBY SMITH

8

Smith went first overall at the 1978 draft and in his 15-year career hit the thousand mark in both games played and points. He won the Cup with Montreal in '86 and ten times scored 20 goals in a season. In his final year with the 67's, he won the scoring title with 192 points, beating runner-up Wayne Gretzky by ten points.

IAN TURNBULL

9

Selected 15th overall at the 1973 draft by the Maple Leafs, Turnbull combined with Borje Salming to create one of the most talented offensive pairings in the league. "Bull" twice scored 20 goals in a season and holds the NHL record for goals by a defenceman in one game — five — a record he set against the Detroit Red Wings.

10 DOUG WILSON

Wilson played three years with the 67's before moving directly into the NHL his draft year. He played more than 1,000 games over three decades, and in 1981–82 scored an incredible 39 goals from the blueline. He played in seven All-Star games and won the Norris Trophy in 1982, though he never won the Stanley Cup.

Doug Wilson

First Ten **SOVIET** Players **DRAFTED** By **NHL** Teams

1 VIKTOR KHATULEV

Philadelphia Flyers   Chosen 160th 1975 Amateur Draft

Dynamo Riga centre Viktor Khatulev became the first Soviet player drafted by an NHL club when the Philadelphia Flyers chose him the summer after they won their second consecutive Stanley Cup. Khatulev never played a game for the Flyers nor did he became an international player of any consequence for the USSR.

2 VIACHESLAV FETISOV

Montreal Canadiens   Chosen 201st 1978 Amateur Draft

Fetisov was an standout junior for the USSR. He became one of the all-time great Soviet players and a star on the international scene. He won six gold medals at the World Championships and three Olympic titles. Fetisov also helped the USSR win the 1981 Canada Cup and was a long-serving captain of the Central Red Army team.

3 VICTOR SHKURDYUK

St. Louis Blues   Chosen 203rd 1978 Amateur Draft

SKA Leningrad right-winger Victor Shkurdyuk never played a game in the NHL nor did he gain any fame on the USSR national squad. His selection did mark the first time two Soviet players were selected in the same draft year.

4 VIKTOR NECHAYEV

Los Angeles Kings   Chosen 132nd 1982 Entry Draft

SKA Leningrad centre Viktor Nechayev made history as a member of the L.A. Kings in 1982–83 when he became the first player drafted from the USSR to play a game and score a goal in the NHL.

5   SERGEI KAPUSTIN

New York Rangers   Chosen 141st 1982 Entry Draft

Left-winger Kapustin scored two goals and one assist in the Soviet Union's victory over the NHL All-Stars in the three-game Challenge Cup series played at Madison Square Garden in 1979. He represented the Soviet Union at the inaugural Canada Cup tournament in 1976 and later recorded an assist in the USSR's 8–1 thrashing of Canada in the 1981 Canada Cup final.

6   VICTOR ZHLUKTOV

Minnesota North Stars   Chosen 143rd 1982 Entry Draft

Left-winger Zhluktov enjoyed an exemplary career with the national team and the Central Red Army. He registered a goal and an assist for the victorious Soviet team in the three-game Challenge Cup. Zhluktov helped the Soviets win the 1981 Canada Cup and appeared in the 1982–83 USSR All-Star Team's tour of the NHL.

7   VLADISLAV TRETIAK

Montreal Canadiens   Chosen 143rd 1983 Entry Draft

A top international player, Tretiak first gained prominence with the USSR squad that narrowly lost to Canada in the 1972 Summit Series. He performed brilliantly in the Red Army's 3–3 tie with the Habs on New Year's Eve 1975, backstopped the USSR to ten World Championships and three Olympic titles, and was chosen tournament MVP after winning the 1981 Canada Cup. In 1989 he became the first Soviet player elected to the Hockey Hall of Fame.

8   VIACHESLAV FETISOV

New Jersey Devils   Chosen 150th 1983 Entry Draft

One of the first players to be drafted twice, Fetisov was a former three-time winner of the Gold Stick Award as Europe's top player and played nearly six seasons with the Devils. In 1994–95 he was traded to Detroit where he helped the team reach the Stanley Cup finals that year. In 1996–97 he contributed to Detroit's first Stanley Cup win since 1954–55. The team repeated in 1998 with Fetisov playing a prominent role once again.

ALEXANDER CHERNYKH

New Jersey Devils   Chosen 192nd 1983 Entry Draft

Chernykh played at the 1988 Calgary Olympics where he helped the USSR win its most recent gold medal. The Devils' cluster of Soviet picks in 1983 carved them a place in history as one of the pioneering teams in terms of the Eastern European influence in the NHL.

10 ALEXEI KASATONOV

New Jersey Devils   Chosen 234th 1983 Entry Draft

Defenceman Kasatonov won Olympic gold twice and was a member of five World Championship teams. In 1981 he was chosen an all-star after helping the USSR win the Canada Cup. Between 1989 and 1996 he scored 160 NHL points with New Jersey, Anaheim, St. Louis, and Boston.

Viacheslav Fetisov

Ten **LATE AMATEUR** Draft Or **ENTRY** Draft **SELECTIONS** To Play In The NHL

1

STEFAN PERSSON

Selected 214th overall by the Islanders in 1974, Persson nonetheless went on to play nine years and 600 games in the NHL, all on Long Island.

2

DAVE TAYLOR

An unbelievable find, Taylor was taken 210th overall by Los Angeles in 1975. Two years later, he scored 20 goals with the Kings, and in 17 seasons with Los Angeles he played 1,111 games, scored 431 goals and 1,069 points.

3

CHRIS NILAN

Not the most talented player, Nilan was selected 231st overall by Montreal in 1978. He played only part of one season in the minors, then lasted nearly 700 games in the NHL, amassing more than 3,000 penalty minutes along the way. He was a member of the 1986 Stanley Cup-winning Canadiens and represented the United States at the 1987 Canada Cup.

4

DOMINIK HASEK

For years, Hasek was an unwanted goalie. Drafted a preposterous 207th in 1983 by Chicago, he played seven years in his native Czechoslovakia before the Hawks gave him a starting assignment in the NHL. After 25 games in the Windy City over two years (1990–92), the Hawks dealt him to Buffalo. The Sabres have never been the same.

5

UWE KRUPP

One of the first German players to be drafted, Krupp went 223rd in 1983 when Buffalo selected him. Three years later, he was with the Sabres where he stayed for six years. He became the first European to score a Stanley Cup-winning goal when he won game four in overtime for Colorado in 1996.

6 KEVIN MILLER

Selected 202nd overall by the Rangers in 1984, Miller played junior with the Michigan State Spartans before joining the Rangers in 1988. In ten NHL seasons he has played for seven teams as a utility forward.

7 IGOR LARIONOV

Another European taken low in the draft because of uncertainty about his availability, Larionov went 214th overall to Vancouver in 1985. He joined the Canucks four years later after a 12-year career in the Soviet Union with Khimik and CSKA Moscow yet has still played 500 games in the NHL and won two Stanley Cups with the Red Wings in Detroit.

8 KEN BAUMGARTNER

"Bomber" has been a survivor and scrapper since being drafted 245th by Buffalo in 1985. He has played with five teams in his 12-year career, and in ten of those seasons has passed 100 penalty minutes. A team leader, he has always been a respected player on the ice, and off the ice he has been involved in the NHLPA for a number of years.

9 VALERI ZELEPUKIN

Selected 221st by New Jersey in 1990, Zelepukin provided almost seven reliable years with the Devils (and one Stanley Cup) before being traded on January 4, 1998, to Edmonton with Bill Guerin for Jason Arnott and Bryan Muir. Twice he scored 20 goals in a season as a left-winger, and in 1998 he played on Russia's silver medal team at the Nagano Olympics.

10 NIKOLAI KHABIBULIN

The "Bulin Wall" was taken a lowly 204th by Winnipeg in 1992 but has improved every year he's been in the league. He now has more than 100 career wins, including 30 or more in each of his last three seasons, and has played for Team Europe in each of the last two NHL All-Star games.

1 BERNIE PARENT
Philadelphia (from Boston)

Parent, of course, became the backbone for the Broad Street Bullies' Stanley Cup wins in 1974 and '75. In both seasons, he won the Vezina and Conn Smythe Trophies, and he was elected into the Hockey Hall of Fame shortly after his career was cut short by an eye injury.

2 BILL GOLDSWORTHY
Minnesota (from Boston)

Goldsworthy played almost ten full seasons with the North Stars after playing just 33 games with the Bruins part-time during the previous three years. He was team captain for two years (1974–76) and after his career was over, the North Stars retired his number 8 jersey.

3 JOE WATSON
Philadelphia (from Boston)

Watson joined the Flyers after playing the previous full season in Boston, and stayed in Philly for the next eleven years, winning two Stanley Cups and playing a solid role on the defence in front of Parent. He never had more than 30 penalty minutes in any season despite being on the most penalized teams in the history of the game.

4 AL ARBOUR
St. Louis (from Toronto)

Arbour played three and a half seasons with the Blues, then became a part-time coach and continued as a player under Scotty Bowman. When the Islanders hired him as their bench boss, he went on to become one of the winningest coaches in the history of the game. A defensive defenceman, he was the only player of his generation to wear glasses, and with Glenn Hall (see below) anchored the team's blueline to three consecutive trips to the Stanley Cup finals.

GLENN HALL
St. Louis (from Chicago)

Like all great goalies, Hall gave the Blues credibility and the chance to win every time he strapped on the pads. He gave players inspiration and experience needed to cope with being a first-year team in the NHL. Hall was one of the main reasons the Blues went to the Stanley Cup finals, and although the team didn't win a single game against 12 successive losses, the post-season success helped establish St. Louis as a hockey city that thrives to this day.

Bill Goldsworthy

Five Players Who **MADE** The
ALL-ROOKIE Team And Then **FIZZLED**

1

IAIN DUNCAN
Winnipeg (1987–88)

Duncan played six games the season before with the Jets, but in
'87–'88 was called up from Moncton (AHL) early in the year and —
for a brief time — never looked back. He had 19 goals and 42
points in his rookie season, and the following year scored 44 points.
But that was as far as he went. He played all of 1989–90 with
Moncton and was called up for two games the next year. Since
then, he has played in the IHL, AHL, ECHL, and CHL.

2

PATRICK LALIME
Pittsburgh (1996–97)

Lalime burst on the scene during the '96–'97 season after playing in
obscurity for the Cleveland Lumberjacks of the IHL. He was called
up to the Penguins after injuries to regulars Tom Barrasso and Ken
Wregget, and promptly went 16 games without a loss to begin his
NHL career, a new league record. However, he wound up going
7–12 in his next 19 games. Barrasso and Wregget returned, and
Lalime was sent to play in the IHL with Grand Rapids.

3

OLEG PETROV
Montreal (1993–94)

Petrov was drafted 127th overall by Montreal in the 1991 draft
and played nine games for the Habs in '92–'93 before making the
grade the next year. However, he spent most of the next two
seasons splitting his time between the big club and the farm team
in Fredericton, and for the last three seasons has skated in
Switzerland (with Ambri-Piotta) and Italy (HC Meran).

GILBERT DIONNE
Montreal (1991–92)

Although he played in only 39 games in '91–'92 when he was drafted by the team, Dionne scored 21 goals and seemed to be just the offensive tonic the Habs needed. But in the next two seasons he scored only 20 and was traded to the Flyers in 1994–95. The Flyers traded Dionne to Florida, and from there he was sent to Carolina of the AHL and then to Cincinnati of the IHL.

KEN HODGE JR.
Boston (1990–91)

Being the son of an NHLer might mean having some advantages along the way, but it also means being expected to equal the achievements of the father. For one brief season, Ken Hodge Jr. fulfilled that hope, scoring 30 goals for Boston in 1990–91. But the next year, he split his time between Boston and the Maine Mariners, and the following summer he was sent to Tampa Bay where he scored just twice in 25 games. His résumé since then is a veritable where's where of the hockey Baedecker: Atlanta Knights, Kansas City Blades, Minnesota Moose, and San Diego Gulls of the IHL; Binghampton Rangers, AHL; Cardiff Lions in Britain and Ratingen Lions of Berlin.

Ten **BEST** Players To **BEGIN** Their Pro Career In The **WORLD HOCKEY ASSOCIATION**

1 WAYNE GRETZKY

Gretzky formalized his pro status by signing with the WHA's Indianapolis Racers as an underage free agent on June 12, 1978. He played his first eight games as a pro for the Racers before he was traded to the Edmonton Oilers where he scored 104 points in 72 games. Gretzky joined the NHL with the Oilers following the merger of the two leagues prior to the 1979–80 season.

2 MARK MESSIER

In November 1978, the Indianapolis Racers signed underage free agent Mark Messier to a ten-game tryout and the Cincinnati Stingers signed him after the Racers franchise folded. Following the NHL-WHA merger in 1979, the Edmonton Oilers chose him 48th overall in the Entry Draft.

Mark Messier

MIKE GARTNER

3 Gartner spent his first pro season with the Stingers in 1978–79 where he scored 27 goals. The Washington Capitals chose him in the 1979 Entry Draft and he recorded four 40-goal seasons. Gartner later played for the Minnesota North Stars, New York Rangers, Toronto Maple Leafs, and Phoenix Coyotes. He retired after the 1997–98 season with 708 career goals and an NHL record fifteen consecutive 30-goal seasons.

MICHEL GOULET

4 The Birmingham Bulls signed Goulet as an underage free agent from the Quebec Remparts of the QMJHL. Following their merger with the NHL, the Quebec Nordiques drafted him 20th overall at the 1979 NHL Entry Draft. Goulet became one of the NHL's top shooters as indicated by his four straight 50-goal seasons between 1982–83 and 1985–86.

MARK HOWE

5 Howe joined the NHL in 1979–80 when the Hartford Whalers became one of four former WHA clubs to merge with its former rival. He was one of the NHL's top defencemen in Hartford and Philadelphia and was placed on the NHL First All-Star team in 1983, 1986, and 1987.

MIKE LIUT

6 Goaltender Mike Liut played two seasons with the Stingers, where he led the league in shutouts during the 1978–79 season. An original draft choice of St. Louis in 1976, Liut was reclaimed by the Blues prior to the 1979 Expansion Draft and led all NHL backstoppers with 33 wins in 1979–80. He closed out his playing career in 1992 with career totals of 25 shutouts, 294 wins, and a 3.49 goals against average.

7 KENT NILSSON

Swedish centre Kent Nilsson recorded consecutive 107-point seasons for the Winnipeg Jets in 1977–78 and 1978–79. Originally drafted by the Atlanta Flames in 1976, he was reacquired by them and experienced little difficulty adjusting to the NHL as indicated by his 40 goals and 93 points in 1979–80. Nilsson concluded his NHL career with 686 points in 553 regular season games.

8 MIKE ROGERS

Rogers played with the WHA's Edmonton Oilers and New England Whalers from 1974–75 to 1978–79 and joined the NHL with the Hartford Whalers in 1979–80, whereupon he registered his first of three consecutive 100-point seasons. The third of these came with the New York Rangers where he played four full seasons. In 484 NHL regular season games Rogers accumulated 519 points.

9 RICK VAIVE

Vaive joined the Birmingham Bulls in 1978–79. After the NHL-WHA merger he was chosen fifth overall by the Vancouver Canucks at the 1979 Entry Draft. During his rookie season he was traded to the Toronto Maple Leafs where his career blossomed. Vaive topped the 30-goal mark seven straight years in Toronto including three consecutive 50-goal years from 1981–82 to 1983–84. He retired in 1992 with 441 goals and 788 points.

10 RICHARD BRODEUR

Brodeur tended goal for the Quebec Nordiques from 1972 to 1979 and led the team to the Avco Cup championship in 1976–77. Following the NHL-WHA merger, he spent a year in the New York Islanders' organization. He was traded to the Vancouver Canucks where he anchored Vancouver's improbable march to the 1982 Stanley Cup finals.

Ten **LEAST-KNOWN** Players To Score A
PLAYOFF HAT TRICK

PERCY GALBRAITH
Boston, March 31, 1927

Galbraith scored his three goals against Hugh Lehman of Chicago in a 4–4 tie. In 30 other playoff games, he scored just once, and in 347 regular season games he had just 29 goals. Lehman, too, was hardly a big name; this was one of only two playoff games in which he tended the twine.

JOE BENÔIT
Montreal, March 22, 1941

Benôit scored six playoff goals in just eleven career games, three against Sam LoPresti in Montreal's 4–3 win over the Hawks. He played just five years in the NHL, from 1940 to 1947; during that time he was in the military for two years. In each of his first three seasons his goals increased, from 16 to 20 to 30, but after returning from war he fell to seasons of nine goals and then none, and was dealt to the Springfield Indians.

GERRY PLAMONDON
Montreal, March 24, 1949

Plamondon had just seven goals in 74 career regular-season games, but in the 1949 playoffs scored five times in seven games, including three against the great Harry Lumley. A career minor-leaguer, Plamondon began in the Montreal junior system and never played a full year with the Habs. He finished his career first in the Quebec Senior league, then with the Pembroke Lumber Kings of the Eastern Ontario Hockey League.

ROSAIRE PAIEMENT
Philadelphia, April 13, 1968

Paiement played three playoff games and scored three goals, all in this one game, one against the great Glenn Hall, the other two against Hall's backup, the famed international Canadian, Seth Martin. Paiement had only 48 goals in 190 NHL games, making his hat trick a rare post-season accomplishment.

5

TOM WILLIAMS

Los Angeles, April 14, 1974

Williams had one big year in the NHL, 1976–77, when he scored 35 goals. Beyond that, he was a left-winger of little note who was drafted 27th overall by the Rangers in 1971. He played in the NHL from 1971–79, then finished his career with the Salt Lake Golden Eagles of the CHL.

6

PAUL HOLMGREN

Philadelphia, May 15, 1980

Holmgren was a goon who spent the majority of his career in the penalty box. However, in 1979–80 he had a career year, scoring 30 goals and then another ten in the playoffs. His hat trick came against Billy Smith in the Flyers' 8–3 hammering of the Islanders in game two of the finals, but the New Yorkers fought back and won the Stanley Cup in six games.

7

JOHN DRUCE

Washington, April 21, 1990

Like so many before him, Druce had one spectacular moment during his career, and for him it was the 1990 playoffs. Drafted 40th overall by Washington in 1985, Druce was in only his second part-time year when the '90 playoffs arrived, and he scored 14 goals in 15 games that spring when the team went to the semifinals. In 37 playoff games over the next decade, he scored just three more times.

8

BRIAN NOONAN

Chicago, April 18, 1993

Noonan was drafted 186th overall by Chicago in 1983, and it was a tribute to his perseverance that he made the NHL at all. His hat trick against Curtis Joseph represented all Chicago's goals in a 4–3 loss. Still in the NHL after eleven seasons, Noonan has never had a 20-goal year, coming closest with 19 in 1991–92.

9 PAUL DiPIETRO
Montreal, April 28, 1993

DiPietro scored three times against Ron Hextall in a 6–2 win over provincial rivals Quebec Nordiques. This was the spring of the team's improbable run to the Cup, and DiPietro's crowning glory in a brief career that lasted only 192 games and 31 goals over six years. Only once did he play a full season (1993–94), and after bouncing around from the big top to the minors, DiPietro retired after finishing '96–'97 with the Cincinnati Cyclones of the IHL.

10 MIKE SULLIVAN
Calgary, May 11, 1995

Sullivan has just four career playoff goals in 24 games, three of them coming against Arturs Irbe and Wade Flaherty in Calgary's 9–2 slaughtering of San Jose, the team that had traded him the previous year. Sullivan has played most of the last seven years in the NHL, but has never scored more than nine goals in any full season.

First Ten Players To Score **FIVE OR MORE GOALS** In A Game

1

JOE MALONE
Montreal Canadiens — December 19, 1917

2

HARRY HYLAND
Montreal Wanderers — December 19, 1917

These two players led their teams to victory on the same night in different games. "Phantom" Joe Malone was one of hockey's first star centres. His nickname referred to the near-impossible task of keeping track of his whereabouts on the ice. Right-winger Hyland was part of the Wanderers' Stanley Cup triumph in 1909–10. He established himself as one of hockey's greatest offensive threats.

3

NEWSY LALONDE
Montreal Canadiens — January 10, 1920

Edouard "Newsy" Lalonde sent five pucks past Toronto Arenas net-minder Ivan Mitchell in a 14–7 romp. Lalonde excelled in hockey's famous early leagues including the Federal Amateur Hockey League the International Hockey League — the first pro league in North America — the National Hockey Association, and the Pacific Coast Hockey Association.

4

MICKEY ROACH
Toronto St. Pats — March 6, 1920

Centre Mickey Roach scored five goals in a game against the Quebec Bulldogs. He spent most of his career with the Hamilton Tigers and was on hand in 1925 when the team became the first in NHL history to go on strike.

5

CORB DENNENY
Toronto St. Pats — January 26, 1921

Denneny victimised Howie Lockhart of the Hamilton Tigers. The centre/left wing played a key role on the Toronto Arenas club that won the Stanley Cup during the first year of the NHL, 1917–18.

Joe Malone

6 CY DENNENY
Ottawa Senators — March 7, 1921

Ottawa left-winger Cy Denneny scored five goals against the Hamilton Tigers. This carved the siblings' place in history as the first set of brothers to record five-goal games. Cy's forte was his deadly accurate shot which allowed him to overcome his below-average skating ability.

7 BABE DYE
Toronto St. Pats — December 16, 1922

Dye was the only player to beat legendary Georges Vézina five times in one game. He enjoyed his most fruitful years with the Toronto St. Pats in the early 1920s, forming one of the game's best forward lines with Corb Denneny and Reg Noble.

8 REDVERS GREEN
Hamilton Tigers — December 5, 1924

Forward Redvers Green recorded a five-goal game against John Ross Roach of the Toronto St. Pats. Green was also part of the Hamilton Tigers' legendary revolt in 1925.

9 HARRY "PUNCH" BROADBENT
Montreal Maroons — January 7, 1925

One could argue that right-winger Broadbent's five-goal game against Vernon Forbes of the Hamilton Tigers was anti-climactic. As a member of the Ottawa Senators three years earlier, Broadbent established an NHL standard by scoring a goal in sixteen consecutive games.

10 PIT LEPINE
Montreal Canadiens — December 14, 1925

The Habs' Pit Lepine drew attention to himself by beating Ottawa Senators goalie Alex Connell five times in one match. He was a key member of Montreal's consecutive Stanley Cup teams in 1930 and 1931.

Ten **LEAST-KNOWN** Players To Have Their **NUMBER RETIRED**

1 **BARRY ASHBEE #4**
Philadelphia Flyers (1970–74)

Ashbee spent most of 1959 to 1970 playing in the minors, the only NHL blip a 14-game stint with Boston in 1965–66. He became a regular on the Flyers' blueline in 1970 at age 31, but played only four years before suffering a career-ending injury in the 1974 Stanley Cup semifinals when he was struck in the eye by a shot by Dale Rolfe of the Rangers. He took a job with the Flyers as an assistant coach, but tragedy struck again when he was diagnosed with leukaemia. He passed away May 12, 1977.

2 **MICHEL BRIÈRE #21**
Pittsburgh Penguins (1969–70)

"Mike" Brière played only one full season with the Penguins, 1969–70, scoring 12 goals and 44 points. A native of Malartic, Quebec, he was the passenger of a vehicle that was involved in a single-car accident on May 15, 1970. The crash caused serious brain damage and he died on April 13, 1971, after never having regained consciousness. A top-notch rookie, he had been considered for the Calder Trophy, along with Tony Esposito and eventual winner, Bobby Clarke.

3 **FRANK FINNIGAN #8**
Ottawa Senators (1924–34)

Called variously the "Shawville Express," the "Shawville Meteor," or the "Shawville Flash" owing to his birthplace and speed, Finnigan had his number retired by the new Senators for two reasons. First, he was an original Senator from 1923–31 and 1932–34 (and captain in 1930–31); second, he played an important role in Ottawa securing an expansion team for 1992. He was asked to drop the puck for the franchise's first game and watch his number raised to the rafters, but he passed away Christmas Day 1991.

4

BOB GASSOFF #3
St. Louis Blues (1973–77)

Gassoff played less than four full years in the NHL, 1973–77, all with the Blues, before his life was cut short in a highway accident. In the summer of 1977, teammate Garry Unger hosted a barbecue at his farm near Gray Summit, Montana. During the afternoon, Gassoff went for a ride on a trail bike. As he drove over a hill he ran head on into a car and died instantly. Prior to the game against Atlanta on October 1, 1977, the Blues retired his number.

5

AL HAMILTON #3
Edmonton Oilers (1972–80)

Hamilton began his career with the Rangers in 1965–66; he stayed for four years before joining the Sabres for two. He jumped to the Alberta (soon to be Edmonton) Oilers, and for seven years was their most dependable defenceman. He was nicknamed "Hard Luck" for good reason. He once broke the same kneecap twice in one year, and in '77–'78 he was hit in the eye by a puck, an accident that nearly ended his career. Hamilton's number was honoured in October, 1980, a few months after he retired.

6

YVON LABRE #7
Washington Capitals (1974–81)

The only player to wear #7 for Washington, Labre played the last seven years of his career with the Caps, from 1974 to 1981, and was team captain from 1975–78. He retired after two serious knee operations. He was voted the Caps' MVP in 1976–77 despite scoring only three times (two were short-handed goals) and had only 101 career points to 788 penalty minutes. His is the only number the Caps have retired.

7

RICK LEY #2
Hartford Whalers (1972–81)

Ley joined the Whalers in their first WHA season, leaving the NHL and the Leafs after four years. He was Hartford's captain for six years, played in the WHA's All-Star game every year, and was named the team's best defenceman in 1978, 1979, and 1980. In 1979, he won the Best Defenceman award in the WHA. He played for the Whalers their first two years in the NHL, 1979–81, and then retired. His number was officially honoured on December 26, 1982.

8 BILL MASTERTON #19
Minnesota North Stars (1967–68)

Masterton is the only NHL player to die as a result of injuries suffered during a game, against California, when he collided with two Seals and hit his head on the ice. He lost consciousness and died two days later, January 15, 1968, the day before the 1968 All-Star game was played. That spring, the NHL introduced the Bill Masterton Trophy, awarded annually to the player "who best exemplifies the qualities of perseverance, sportsmanship, and dedication to hockey." His number wasn't officially retired by the Minnesota North Stars until 1987, but no Minnesota player ever wore #19 after the accident.

9 JOHN McKENZIE #19
Hartford Whalers (1976–79)

McKenzie played just two and a half years with the Whalers. His honour was as much for his contribution to the NHL as to the WHA team. He played for all four U.S.-based Original Six teams, winning the Stanley Cup with Boston in 1970 and '72 during five NHL seasons before joining the Philadelphia Blazers in 1972. He also played for Vancouver, Minnesota, and Cincinnati before joining New England midway through the '76–'77 season. His number was retired by Hartford on February 27, 1980, the first Whaler so honoured.

10 STAN SMYL #12
Vancouver Canucks (1978–91)

Stan Smyl holds many of Vancouver's franchise records, the result of playing all of his 13 NHL seasons with the Canucks (1978–91). He was the captain for eight years ('82–'90) and played more games (896), scored more goals, assists, and points (262, 411, 673) than any other member of Vancouver. In honour of his dedication to the team, his number was the first Canuck jersey to be officially retired, on November 3, 1991.

Ten **LESSER-KNOWN** Players To Wear The **NUMBER** Of A **GREAT** **PLAYER** Who Followed

1

AL LANGLOIS

Langlois had a pedestrian career in the NHL, playing for four teams between 1957 and 1966. His last stop was Boston, and there the defenceman wore #4 for one year before retiring. The next year, his number was taken by Bobby Orr.

2

ROY CONACHER

Conacher played only one season with the Detroit Red Wings, 1946–47, his first full year back in the NHL after three years in the RCAF. That season, he wore #9, and a rookie teammate of his wore #17. The next year, Conacher was sold to Chicago, and that teammate, Gordie Howe, slipped comfortably into the number 9 sweater.

3

LORNE CARR

Carr began his Leaf life in 1941 after being acquired from the Brooklyn Americans, and he wore #9 during his stay with the Leafs. He retired after the '45–'46 season, and teammate Ted Kennedy, who had been wearing #12, adopted the more familiar #9.

4

PIT MARTIN

Martin's last year with the Bruins was 1966–67, after which he was traded to Chicago, where he spent most of the last dozen years of his career. His number 7 was picked up by newcomer Phil Esposito, who had been acquired from Chicago in the same deal.

5

TOD SLOAN

"Slinker" Sloan played most of his career in Toronto, but in 1958–59 he was sold to Chicago, where he wore #9. The next year, he changed numbers, and second-year man Bobby Hull took #9.

CHARLIE SANDS

6 Sands played more than a dozen years in the NHL, including 1939–43 with Les Canadiens, wearing #9. He was loaned to the Rangers the next year, and rookie Maurice Richard took #9 as his own. No Hab has worn the number since.

IVAN IRWIN

7 Irwin played just four games with Montreal in 1952–53 and was traded to the Rangers in the summer where he played bits and pieces of four more seasons. While with the Canadiens, he wore #4, but the next year newcomer Jean Beliveau, a forward, adopted the defender's number.

Ivan Irwin

GORD NELSON

8 Nelson was signed as a free agent by the Leafs on December 10, 1969, and during his uneventful three games with the team wore #27. The next year, first-round draft choice Darryl Sittler stepped into #27 and wore it proudly for the next decade.

IVAN BOLDIREV AND RANDY LADOUCEUR

9 Both Ladouceur and Boldirev wore #19 in 1982–83 for the Red Wings, Boldirev the last half of the year after being acquired from Vancouver in January '83. Although both men stayed with the Wings the following season, Boldirev reverted to his more familiar #12 and Ladouceur to #29, paving the way for rookie Steve Yzerman to take #19.

KELLY KISIO

10 The timing couldn't have been better planned. Kisio wore #11 on Broadway for five years, but was traded in the summer of 1991 to San Jose. That same summer, the Rangers signed Mark Messier as a free agent, and Messier was able to adopt the number he made famous in Edmonton.

1

WAYNE CASHMAN

Cashman was a hard-nosed right-winger who racked up 793 career points in 1,027 regular season games for the Boston Bruins after joining the team full time in 1968–69. By the early 1970s he formed one of the league's top forward lines with Phil Esposito and Ken Hodge and helped Boston win the Stanley Cup in 1970 and 1972.

2

WAYNE STEPHENSON

Stephenson was a solid netminder who played 328 regular season games for St. Louis, Philadelphia, and Washington between 1971–72 and 1980–81. He was best known as Bernie Parent's understudy in Philadelphia. When Parent was injured in 1975–76, Stephenson stepped in to win 40 games in 66 appearances for the Flyers.

3

WAYNE THOMAS

Netminder Wayne Thomas played in 243 regular season games for Montreal, Toronto, and the New York Rangers from 1972–73 to 1980–81. He played 52 games for Montreal then joined Toronto in 1975–76 where he enjoyed his best NHL season with 28 wins and an appearance in the NHL All-Star Game.

4

WAYNE BABYCH

A scoring star with Edmonton and Portland of the WCJHL, Babych was the third player chosen in the 1978 Amateur Draft by the St. Louis Blues. He scored 27 goals as a rookie in 1978–79. In 1980–81 Babych had 54 goals playing on one of the NHL's top lines with Bernie Federko and Brian Sutter. Injuries hindered his goal scoring and he retired in 1987 with 192 goals in 519 regular season games.

WAYNE MERRICK

Merrick was chosen 9th overall in the 1972 Amateur Draft by St. Louis after a solid three-year career with the Ottawa 67's of the OHL. He hit the 20-goal mark twice for the Blues then recorded a personal best of 32 goals with St. Louis and California in 1975–76. He filled an important checking role for the N.Y. Islanders when they won four straight Stanley Cups from 1980 to 1983.

WAYNE CARLETON

As a junior with the Toronto Marlboros, left-winger Wayne Carleton won the Memorial Cup in 1964. He enjoyed his best year in Boston in 1970–71 when he scored 22 goals and helped the team finish at the top of the regular season standings.

WAYNE PRESLEY

Presley was a solid two-way right-winger who totalled 302 points in 684 regular season games. He was a key defensive player for Chicago and managed 32- and 21-goal seasons. He later played for San Jose, Buffalo, the New York Rangers, and Toronto before retiring with 155 goals in 684 regular season games.

1

GLENN HALL   OCTOBER 3, 1931

Counting his first two seasons in Detroit, Hall played every game for seven straight years to establish the NHL record for consecutive minutes played. After leading Chicago to a first-place finish in the 1966–67 regular season standings, Hall played for the expansion St. Louis Blues.

2

BILL COOK   OCTOBER 9, 1896

Cook was one of the greatest right-wingers to ever play in the WCHL and the NHL. He spent his entire career with the New York Rangers where he formed the potent "Bread Line" with his brother Bun and Frank Boucher. Cook was a key ingredient in the Blueshirts' first two Stanley Cup triumphs in 1928 and 1933 and twice led the league in scoring.

3

ROY WORTERS   OCTOBER 19, 1900

One of hockey's top goalies during the 1920s and 1930s, Worters turned pro when the Pittsburgh Pirates joined the NHL in 1925–26 and led all league netminders in games played in 1926–27 and 1927–28. "Shrimp" was the first goalkeeper to earn the Hart Trophy and he won the Vezina Trophy in 1931 after posting a league low 1.61 goals against mark.

4

JEAN RATELLE   OCTOBER 3, 1940

Ratelle's greatest scoring exploits came as centre of the "Goal-a-Game (GAG) Line" with Rod Gilbert and Vic Hadfield in the early 1970s. In 1971–72 he registered a personal-high of 109 points and was the winner of the Lester B. Pearson Award. Ratelle also earned his first of two Lady Byng Awards. He was traded to Boston in 1975–76 as part of the Phil Esposito deal. Ratelle played nearly six years in Beantown before retiring in 1980–81 with 491 goals and 1,267 points.

CLINT BENEDICT   SEPTEMBER 26, 1892

5 Benedict was one of hockey's first superstar goalkeepers. He won three Stanley Cups with the Ottawa Senators and a fourth with the Montreal Maroons. In Montreal he experimented briefly with a piece of protective equipment over his nose but soon discarded it. Benedict retired in 1930 with a 2.32 goals against average, 57 shutouts, and 191 career wins.

FRANK BOUCHER   OCTOBER 7, 1901

6 One of hockey's classiest players, Boucher was granted permanent possession of the original Lady Byng Trophy after he won the award seven times in eight years. He gained fame as the centre between Bill and Bun Cook on the legendary "Bread Line." Boucher helped the Rangers win the Stanley Cup in 1928 and 1933 and was named to the NHL First All-Star Team three times. He recorded 423 points in 557 regular season games.

GRANT FUHR   SEPTEMBER 28, 1962

7 Fuhr's spectacular talent was a key reason behind the Edmonton Oilers' success and formed an outstanding netminding tandem with Andy Moog from 1981–82 to 1986–87. In 1988 he won the Vezina Trophy and was placed on the NHL First All-Star Team. In the 1990s Fuhr moved on to Toronto, Buffalo, Los Angeles, and St. Louis.

PATRICK ROY   OCTOBER 5, 1965

8 As a rookie in 1986, Roy won the Conn Smythe Trophy after leading the Montreal Canadiens to the Stanley Cup. He continued to excel in the Montreal net where he won three Vezina Trophies in four years between 1989 and 1992. In 1992–93, Roy led Montreal to another Stanley Cup and earned his second Conn Smythe Trophy. In 1995 he was traded to Colorado where he won a third Stanley Cup.

9 FRANK BRIMSEK   SEPTEMBER 26, 1915

Brimsek was one of the first significant NHL players born in the United States. He played all but one of his seasons with the Boston Bruins where he won two Stanley Cups. "Mr. Zero" was particularly stingy in the 1939 finals when he held the Toronto Maple Leafs to only six goals in the five-game series. Brimsek recorded 40 shutouts, 252 wins, and a 2.70 goals against average.

10 LORNE CHABOT   OCTOBER 5, 1900

After helping the Port Arthur Bearcats win consecutive Allan Cups in 1925 and 1926, goaltender Lorne Chabot broke in with the New York Rangers in 1926–27. The following season he helped the Blueshirts win their first Stanley Cup. He also won another Stanley Cup with Toronto in 1932, captured the Vezina Trophy as a member of Chicago in 1935, and was the losing goaltender when the Maroons dropped the longest playoff game in history to Detroit in 1936.

Jean Ratelle

1

STEVE **BANCROFT**

Bancroft, born in Toronto, played just one game in
the NHL, with Chicago in 1992–93, though he was originally Leaf
property. He was traded five times and was owned by Boston,
Chicago, Winnipeg, Florida, and Pittsburgh, as well as the Leafs.

2

LEN **BARRIE**

Barrie struggled to make it to the NHL despite leading
the WHL with 185 points in his final year of junior. He was drafted
by Edmonton in 1988 but played only sparingly with Philadelphia,
Pittsburgh, and Florida before moving to Europe to play. In 64
career games, he has five goals.

3

BRANDON CONVERY

Born in Kingston, Ontario, Convery was drafted by the
Leafs eighth overall in 1992. He played bits of only two seasons
with them before being traded to Vancouver for Lonny Bohonos on
March 7, 1998.

4

DALLAS EAKINS

Born in Dade City, Florida, Eakins has played with
numerous NHL teams, including Florida and Winnipeg twice each.
In all, he has played only about 100 NHL games in seven seasons
since being drafted by Washington in 1985.

5

JASON **HOLLAND**

Born in Morinville, Alberta, Holland fought hard to stay
with the New York Islanders, playing just 12 games in the last two
years before being traded to Buffalo with Paul Kruse for Jason Dawe.

6

CHAD KILGER

Kilger was drafted fourth overall by Anaheim in 1995 but
was part of the huge trade with Winnipeg that involved Teemu
Selanne and Oleg Tverdovsky in 1995–96. After splitting the next
year between the relocated Phoenix Coyotes and the farm, Kilger was
traded to Chicago, where he has struggled with a last-place team.

NATHAN **LAFAYETTE**

7

Born in New Westminster, British Columbia, Lafayette has played only parts of the last five seasons in the NHL, playing more in the minors than the bigs. For three successive seasons he was traded during the year, from St. Louis to Vancouver (1993–94), Vancouver to the Rangers ('94–'95), and the Rangers to Los Angeles (1995–96). He is now in his third year with the Kings but has yet to become a regular with the team.

GAETANO **ORLANDO**

8

Although drafted by Buffalo in 1981, Orlando played just 98 games with the Sabres from 1984 to 1987 before embarking on a long European career that continues some dozen years later. He was born in Montreal, but because of dual citizenship has also been able to represent Italy at nine World Championships and two Olympics (1994 and 1998).

BOB **PARADISE**

9

Undrafted, Paradise was signed by Montreal in 1970 before being traded to Minnesota, where he began his NHL career. In eight NHL seasons, he played 368 games and scored 62 points. He was traded five times, including twice to Pittsburgh, where he finished his career in 1978–79.

Ten NHL Players **BORN** In
UNIQUE PLACES

RICK CHARTRAW
Caracas, Venezuela

The Montreal Canadiens made Chartraw the tenth player chosen in the 1974 Amateur Draft. A tough, stay-at-home defenceman, Chartraw played a part in the Habs' four consecutive Stanley Cup championships between 1976 and 1979.

2

MIKE GREENLAY
Vitoria, Brazil

Goalie Mike Greenlay enjoyed a solid amateur career with Lake Superior State University and the Saskatoon Blades of the WHL where he played in the 1989 Memorial Cup. He made two appearances with the Edmonton Oilers in 1989–90.

3

ED HATOUM
Beirut, Lebanon

Right-winger Ed Hatoum was recruited by the Detroit Red Wings and played 21 games with the parent club in 1968–69 and 1969–70 before he was chosen by the Vancouver Canucks in the 1970 Expansion Draft. Hatoum played 26 games with the Canucks in their inaugural season.

4

OLAF KOLZIG
Johannesburg, South Africa

Netminder Olaf Kolzig was the Washington Capitals' first-round pick, 19th overall, in the 1989 NHL Entry Draft. His breakthrough year was in 1997–98 when he played in 64 games and led the Caps to 33 wins and a place in the Stanley Cup finals for the first time in franchise history.

ROD LANGWAY
Maag, Formosa

As a rookie Langway was an important player on the Habs' blueline when the team won its fourth straight Stanley Cup in 1978–79. After four strong years in Montreal, he went to Washington where he solidified that club's defence and won two Norris Trophies.

Olaf Kolzig

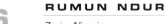

RUMUN NDUR
Zaria, Nigeria

Since 1995 defenceman Rumun Ndur has apprenticed in the AHL while earning three call-ups from the Buffalo Sabres. He remained a prospect in the organization where he began the 1998–99 season before he was sent to the New York Rangers.

WILLI PLETT
Paraguay, South America

Plett scored 33 goals for the Atlanta Flames in 1976–77 and was the recipient of the Calder Trophy. He remained with the Flames franchise through its relocation to Calgary then spent five years in Minnesota and one in Boston before retiring in 1988.

POUL POPEIL
Sollested, Denmark

Between 1965 and 1972 defenceman Poul Popeil played in the minors as well as with Boston, Los Angeles, Detroit, and Vancouver. In 1972–73 he joined the Houston Aeros of the WHA. Popeil retired in 1982.

GRAEME TOWNSEND
Kingston, Jamaica

Right-winger Graeme Townsend was signed as a free agent by the Boston Bruins in 1989. He played 45 regular season games for Boston, the New York Islanders, and Ottawa Senators. He spent most of his time in the AHL, IHL, and Western Professional Hockey League.

CLAUDE VILGRAIN
Port-au-Prince, Haiti

Right-winger Claude Vilgrain spent three years with the Université de Moncton before joining the Canadian National Team. He represented Canada at the 1988 Calgary Olympics and made his NHL debut with the Vancouver Canucks later that season. Vilgrain retired in 1996.

Five Significant Hockey **FIGURES BORN**
In The **UNITED KINGDOM**

1

LORD STANLEY OF PRESTON
Born 1841   London, England

Canada's Governor-General from 1888 to 1893, Frederick Arthur, Lord Stanley of Preston was intrigued by the game of ice hockey. Before leaving office, he donated a trophy to represent hockey supremacy in the Dominion. Originally known as the Dominion Hockey Challenge Cup, the Stanley Cup was sought by amateur players. Following the advent of professionalism in the sport the Cup remained the ultimate prize for teams across North America.

2

FRANK CALDER
Born November 17, 1877   Bristol, England

Calder was the first President of the National Hockey League and served from 1917 to 1943. During his tenure the Boston Bruins, Chicago Blackhawks, Detroit Red Wings, and New York Rangers were added to the league. Each year the Calder Memorial Trophy is awarded to the NHL's most proficient rookie and the Calder Cup is presented to the playoff champion in the American Hockey League.

3

CHUCK GARDINER
Born December 31, 1904   Edinburgh, Scotland

During his seven-year NHL career as a goalie with the Chicago Blackhawks, Gardiner won the Vezina Trophy twice and was a three-time selection to the NHL First All-Star team. His career was cut short following his untimely death from a brain tumour in June 1934. He recorded 42 career shutouts and 112 wins and was elected to the Hockey Hall of Fame in 1945.

4

JOE HALL
Born May 3, 1882   Staffordshire, England

One of hockey's first hard-hitting defencemen, "Bad" Joe Hall won consecutive Stanley Cups with the Quebec Bulldogs in 1912 and 1913. His sudden death from the influenza epidemic in 1918–19 forced the only cancellation of the Stanley Cup final series. Hall was elected to the Hockey Hall of Fame in 1961.

FRED WAGHORNE

Born 1866   Tunbridge Wells, England

One of the game's most innovative on-ice officials, Fred Waghorne implemented the use of a whistle rather than the traditional hand-bell to stop play. He also initiated the rule of dropping the puck for face-offs as opposed to placing it directly on the ice. He was elected to the Hockey Hall of Fame in the Officials Category in 1961.

Fred Waghorne

1

JAMES **BLACK**

A native of Regina, Black has played for Hartford, Minnesota, Dallas, Buffalo, and Chicago in a career that started in 1989. Drafted that summer, 94th overall by the Whalers, he made the team his first camp. He was traded to Minnesota on September 3, 1992, for Mark Janssens, and to Buffalo the following winter with a seventh-round draft choice (Steve Webb) for Gord Donnelly. In seven NHL seasons, though, he has played just 134 games, scoring 23 goals and 47 points.

2

JOHN **BLUE**

Drafted 197th overall by the Winnipeg Jets in 1986, Blue, a goalie, was a career minor leaguer before retiring at the end of the '96–'97 season. He played three years with the University of Minnesota before the draft and most of the next five seasons in the ECHL, IHL, and AHL. He was traded to the North Stars for a seventh-round draft choice in 1988 (Markus Akerblom) but did not make it to the NHL until Boston signed him as a free agent on August 1, 1991. From 1992 to 1994 he appeared in 41 games for the Bruins. In '95–'96, he played just five games for the Sabres and retired at season's end.

3

JEFF **BROWN**

The most current and senior of many Browns to play in the NHL, Jeff has been in the NHL for 13 years with Quebec, St. Louis, Vancouver, and Hartford. Capable offensively, he has 556 career points in 687 games, peaking in '92–'93 when he had 25 goals and 78 points with the Blues. He was with the Canucks in '93–'94 when the team met the Rangers in the Stanley Cup finals, and in 85 career playoff games he has 63 points.

4

GARNET "ACE" BAILEY

Bailey played for four NHL teams, starting with Boston in 1968–69 before being traded to Detroit with a player to be named later (Murray Wing) for Gary Doak on March 1, 1973. He was sent to St. Louis the following year with Ted Harris and Bill

Peter White

Collins for Chris Evans, Bryan Watson, and Jean Hamel on February 14, 1974. The following season he was again dealt, this time to Washington with Stan Gilbertson for Denis Dupere. He ended his career playing with Edmonton in the WHA for one year, 1978–79.

5 TERRY **GRAY**

A native of Montreal, Gray was a career minor leaguer who played professionally for 15 seasons. In that time, he was in the NHL for only 147 games, 42 with Boston, four with Montreal, 65 with Los Angeles, and 38 with St. Louis. He played a number of years in the CHL, AHL, EPHL, and QHL, but the only time he was ever involved in a trade in pro hockey was June 11, 1968, when he went to the Blues from the Kings for Myron Stankiewicz.

6 TRAVIS **GREEN**

Green was selected 23rd overall by the Islanders in the 1989 Entry Draft and finally cracked the team's lineup in 1992. In his rookie season, he played 61 games and scored 25 points, but his team has missed the playoffs the last four years. As a result, he played for Team Canada at the World Championships the past two years and was part of the gold medal team in 1997.

7 **RED** KELLY

The most famous of all players nicknamed "Red," Kelly won eight Stanley Cups (four with Toronto, four with Detroit) and was elected to the Hockey Hall of Fame in 1969. He won the Lady Byng Trophy four times (1951, 1953, 1954, 1961) and the Norris Trophy in '53–'54, and like most everyone so nicknamed he had fire-red hair in his playing days.

8 PETER **WHITE**

White played parts of three seasons with the Edmonton Oilers before being traded to Toronto with a fourth-round draft choice (Jason Sessa) for Kent Manderville. Wearing #18, he played one game with the Leafs before being demoted to their farm team in St. John's. Signed as a free agent in the summer of '96 by the Flyers, he played the next year with the team's AHL affiliate, also in Philadelphia, leading the league in scoring with 105 points and earning a spot on the Second All-Star team.

You Can Make A Player Out Of
VIRTUALLY ANYTHING

1 BOB **CHRYSTAL**
Chrystal was a rugged defenceman who spent the
1953–54 and 1954–55 seasons with the New York Rangers. He
scored 11 goals and 25 points while adding a physical presence to
the Rangers' blueline and played his last four seasons with four
different WHL franchises, where he was a two-time all-star before
retiring in 1959.

2 BALDY **COTTON**
William Harold "Baldy" Cotton played 503 NHL games
on left-wing for three NHL clubs. After nearly five seasons in
Western Pennsylvania, Cotton was traded to Toronto where he was
part of the first Maple Leafs Stanley Cup winner in 1932. His last
two NHL years, from 1935 to 1937, were spent with the New York
Americans. He ended his career with 101 goals and 204 points.

3 JOHN **FLESCH**
Left-winger John Flesch entered the NHL with the
Minnesota North Stars in 1974–75 and played 90 games for the
team over two seasons. In February 1978 he signed as a free agent
with Pittsburgh. He played 124 regular season games and totalled
18 goals and 41 points.

4 BILL **HAY**
Hay joined the Chicago Blackhawks in 1959–60 when
he registered 55 points and was presented the Calder Trophy.
During his last NHL season he helped Chicago finish at the top of
the regular season standings for the first time in three decades.

5 BRUCE **SHOEBOTTOM**
Rugged defenceman Bruce Shoebottom made his NHL
debut when he signed with Boston before the 1987–88 season.
Between 1987 and 1991 he played 35 games on the Bruins'
blueline.

6 DAVE **SILK**

Silk was part of the "Miracle On Ice" U.S. Olympic Team at Lake Placid in 1980. After the improbable gold medal win, he joined the New York Rangers who had originally drafted him 59th overall in 1978. Silk also played for Boston, Detroit, and Winnipeg. In 249 NHL games he scored 54 goals and 113 points.

7 GARTH **SNOW**

Netminder Garth Snow played four years with the University of Maine and appeared with the U.S. Olympic team at Lillehammer in 1994. He saw his first steady action in the NHL with Philadelphia where he played in 90 games over three seasons. In 1997–98 Snow was traded to Vancouver and played in 65 games in 1998–99.

8 STEVE **STONE**

Right-winger Steve Stone amassed 145 points in two seasons with the Niagara Falls Flyers of the OHA but could not maintain the same level of success in the NHL. Stone's NHL tenure consisted of a two-game stint with Vancouver in 1973–74. He spent most of his pro career in the IHL with the Des Moines Oak Leafs and the Port Huron Flags.

9 PAUL **WOODS**

Woods was a reliable playmaking right winger who played 501 regular season games with the Detroit Red Wings from 1977–78 to 1983–84. He was selected to represent Canada at the 1979 World Championships. Woods retired with 72 goals and 196 points.

10 JASON **WOOLLEY**

Defenceman Jason Woolley played in 37 games for the Washington Capitals over three seasons before he was signed as a free agent by the Florida Panthers in February 1995. He also played for Pittsburgh before joining Buffalo. In 1998–99 he was the Sabres co-leader in scoring when the team reached the Stanley Cup finals.

Seven Best Players With **TWO** FIRST NAMES

1

JEAN-CLAUDE TREMBLAY

Tremblay split two years between the Montreal Canadiens and the Eastern Professional Hockey League before gaining a permanent place in the NHL in 1961–62. He scored 363 points in 794 regular season matches and helped Montreal win the Stanley Cup five times.

2

JEAN-PAUL PARISE

Left-winger Jean-Paul Parise played briefly with Boston and Toronto before becoming a fixture in the Minnesota North Stars' line-up from 1967–75. He was a member of Team Canada for the 1972 Summit Series versus the USSR. In 1974–75 he was traded to the New York Islanders. He retired with 238 goals and 594 points in 890 regular season contests.

3

JEAN-GUY GENDRON

Gendron was a dependable left-winger who hit the 20-goal mark twice for the Boston Bruins then played with the Philadelphia Flyers. He registered 383 NHL points before playing his final two years with the Quebec Nordiques in the WHA.

4

LARS-ERIK SJOBERG

Sjoberg was a veteran of the Swedish National Team and domestic league when he joined the Winnipeg Jets of the WHA in 1974–75. He starred with several clubs and represented his country at the 1968 and 1972 Olympics, in five World Championships and at the inaugural Canada Cup in 1976. Sjoberg helped the Jets win the Avco Cup as WHA champions in 1976, 1978, and 1979 and remained with them for one season in 1979–80 after they joined the NHL.

5

VELI-PEKKA KETOLA

A veritable legend in his native Finland, centre Veli-Pekka Ketola was a productive offensive player blessed with good size. He wore the national colours at the 1968 and 1972 Olympics as well as seven World Championships and the Canada Cup in 1976 and

1981. Ketola played three years with the WHA's Winnipeg Jets then 44 games with the Colorado Rockies in 1981–82 scoring nine goals and 14 points.

6 JEAN-PIERRE BORDELEAU

Steady right-winger J.P. Bordeleau played nearly a decade with the Chicago Blackhawks. He was drafted by the Hawks 13th overall in the 1969 Amateur Draft. Beginning in 1972–73 he remained a regular with Chicago until 1980 when he retired with 223 career points.

7 PER-OLAV BRASAR

Left-winger Per-Olav Brasar spent five years in the NHL between 1977–78 and 1981–82. He was at his most productive with the Canucks in 1980–81 when he scored 22 goals and 63 points. The next year he was a part of Vancouver's dramatic run to the Stanley Cup finals.

Lars-Erik Sjober

1 SYL APPS

Apps was a superb two-way centre who twice led the NHL in assists including his first year after which he was presented the Calder Trophy. He also won the Lady Byng Trophy in 1942 and retired in 1948 with 432 points in 423 regular season matches. He was elected to the Hockey Hall of Fame in 1961.

2 GEORGE ARMSTRONG

Armstrong wore Syl Apps' old number 10 with pride from 1953–54 to 1970–71, served as the Leafs' captain from 1957–58 to 1968–69, and helped the club win four Stanley Cups in the 1960s. He racked up 713 career points and was elected to the Hockey Hall of Fame in 1975.

3 BILL COWLEY

Cowley broke into the NHL with the St. Louis Eagles in 1934–35 then was acquired by the Boston Bruins where he played the remainder of his career. He was a two-time winner of the Hart Trophy and claimed the Art Ross Trophy once. Cowley's number 10 was retired by the Boston Bruins and he was elected to the Hockey Hall of Fame in 1968.

4 ALEX DELVECCHIO

Delvecchio was a supreme playmaker during his 24 NHL seasons with the Detroit Red Wings. He was a three-time winner of the Lady Byng Trophy. Delvecchio retired in 1974 with 456 goals and 1,281 points in 1,549 regular season games. His number was retired by the Detroit Red Wings and he was elected to the Hockey Hall of Fame in 1977.

5 RON FRANCIS

Francis topped the 90–point mark three times and helped the Hartford Whalers reach the Adams Division Final in 1986. He was traded to Pittsburgh late in the 1990–91 season in time to contribute to the team's first-ever Stanley Cup win.

6 FRANK FOYSTON

Foyston wore number 10 for the expansion Detroit Cougars in 1926–27 and 1927–28. He was a member of the 1914 Stanley Cup champion Toronto Blueshirts and in 1925 he won the Stanley Cup while playing for the Victoria Cougars. Foyston was elected to the Hockey Hall of Fame in 1958.

7 DALE HAWERCHUK

Hawerchuk was number 10 on the Winnipeg Jets, Buffalo Sabres, St. Louis Blues, and Philadelphia Flyers during his exemplary 17-year career. He won the Calder Trophy in 1982 after scoring 103 points. In all, Hawerchuk topped the 100-point mark six times and finished with 518 goals and 1,409 points.

8 TOM JOHNSON

Defenceman Tom Johnson's number 10 was a fixture in the Montreal Canadiens' line-up during the 1950s and early 1960s. He helped the team win six Stanley Cups and was the 1959 recipient of the Norris Trophy. He retired with 264 points in 978 regular season matches and was elected to the Hockey Hall of Fame in 1970.

9 GUY LAFLEUR

Lafleur led the NHL in scoring three straight years from 1976 to 1978, was a two-time winner of the Hart Trophy and won the 1977 Conn Smythe Trophy. He won four Stanley Cups in Montreal and recorded 560 goals and 1,353 points before retiring in 1991. He was elected to the Hockey Hall of Fame in 1988 and his number was retired by the Montreal Canadiens.

10 BILL MOSIENKO

Mosienko spent his entire career with the Chicago Blackhawks from 1941–42 to 1954–55. He scored 258 career goals including an NHL record three in 21 seconds against the New York Rangers on March 23, 1952. He was the 1945 winner of the Lady Byng Trophy and was elected to the Hockey Hall of Fame in 1965.

Nine **COACHES** With The **SHORTEST** **TERM** Of Duty

1

ROGER CROZIER

Crozier was hired by Washington on a very interim basis, replacing fired Gary Green on November 5, 1981. He was behind the bench for only one game, a loss, and six days later Bryan Murray was hired as the full-time bench boss.

2

DICK DUFF

Duff coached the Leafs for two losses after incumbent Floyd Smith was injured in a car crash. Duff was officially replaced by Punch Imlach, though it was Joe Crozier who assumed duties behind the bench during the games.

3

GORD FASHOWAY

When Bert Olmstead's Oakland Seals were mired in a slump during the 1967–68 season, he retired to the press box for ten games and put Fashoway behind the bench. The strategy didn't seem to work, as the Seals went 4–5–1 during that stretch and finished the season last overall with a 15– 42–17 record.

4

MAURICE FILION

As GM of the Nordiques, Filion hired himself as coach in 1980–81, but after six games and a 1–3–2 start to the season, he stepped down and hired Michel Bergeron as the team's head coach for the remainder of the year.

5

TED GARVIN

Officially, Garvin coached the Red Wings to a 2–8–1 record in eleven games at the start of the '73–'74 season. This awful start led to his firing and the hiring of player Alex Delvecchio as the new coach. However, the NHL no longer allowed player-coaches, so Delvecchio was forced to retire as a player before he could step behind the bench as the coach.

Rogie Vachon

6 TED LINDSAY

The great Hall of Fame player was hired by Detroit in the summer of 1980 amid much fanfare, but the buoyant feelings didn't last long. The Red Wings started the '80–'81 season a dismal 3–14–3, and Lindsay was replaced quickly by Wayne Maxner.

7 RICK PATERSON

Paterson was a stopgap link between the outgoing coach of the '97–'98 Tampa Bay Lightning, Terry Crisp, and the newcomer, Jacques Demers. He was coach for only eight games, and lost each and every one of them.

8 BOB PLAGER

Plager was one of the most popular Blues of all time, but his coaching career lasted just eleven games at the start of the '92–'93 season. He was replaced by Bob Berry who led the team to a 33–30–10 regular-season record and took the Blues to game seven of the division finals against Toronto.

9 ROGIE VACHON

As general manager of the Kings in Los Angeles, Vachon three times fired his coaches and took over on an interim basis. The first time, in '83–'84, was for two games, until he hired Roger Neilson; the second time was for one game after firing Mike Murphy and before hiring Robbie Ftorek; and the third time for seven games came after he fired Barry Melrose.

Ten Best Montreal **CANADIENS** Born In The **UNITED STATES**

1 **CHRIS CHELIOS   CHICAGO, ILLINOIS**
Defenceman Chris Chelios played with the University of Wisconsin then spent a year with the U.S. National team. He joined Montreal in 1984 and helped them upset Boston and Quebec on the way to the Stanley Cup semifinals. Chelios won the Norris Trophy in 1989 when he helped the Habs reach the Stanley Cup finals.

2 **JOHN LeCLAIR   ST. ALBANS, VERMONT**
Power-forward John LeClair represented the United States at the World Junior Championships in 1988 and 1989. He was drafted by Montreal and scored two overtime goals when the Habs beat Los Angeles in the 1993 finals.

3 **MIKE KARAKAS   AURORA, MINNESOTA**
Goalie Mike Karakas played most of his nine-year career with the Chicago Blackhawks where he won a Stanley Cup in 1938. In 1939–40 he played five games for the Canadiens on a special loan from Chicago. The 1936 Calder Trophy winner retired in 1946 with 114 wins and 28 shutouts.

4 **BILL NYROP   WASHINGTON, D.C.**
Defenceman Bill Nyrop played 165 games spread over three seasons for Montreal. His steady play was never more evident than in the 1976, 1977, and 1978 playoffs when the Canadiens won the Stanley Cup. Nyrop died of cancer on New Year's Day 1996.

5 **MATHIEU SCHNEIDER   NEW YORK, N.Y.**
Schneider joined the Habs after a stellar junior career with the Cornwall Royals of the OHL. He contributed to the team's Stanley Cup triumph in 1993 then recorded his first 20-goal season the following year. Schneider played for Team USA when it won the World Cup in 1996.

6   HARRY MUMMERY   CHICAGO, ILLINOIS

Defender Harry Mummery played with the Canadiens when the team was still in the National Hockey Association in 1916–17 and later when it was part of the NHL. His physical presence helped Montreal reach the Stanley Cup final series against eventual champion Seattle in 1917. He spent his final two years in the league with the Hamilton Tigers.

7   CHRIS NILAN   BOSTON, MASSACHUSETTS

Nilan played seven years with the Canadiens and was a part of the 1986 Stanley Cup team. He also skated for the Rangers and Bruins before returning to the Habs late in his final year in 1991–92. Although he piled up over 3,000 minutes in penalties, Nilan managed to record 110 goals and 225 points.

8   CRAIG LUDWIG   RHINELANDER, WISCONSIN

Ludwig joined Montreal after spending three years with the University of North Dakota. He spent eight years in a Habs uniform including the 1985–86 Stanley Cup championship season. Ludwig finished the 1998–99 schedule with 222 points in 1,256 regular season games.

9   TOM KURVERS   MINNEAPOLIS, MINNESOTA

Kurvers joined Montreal in 1984–85 out of the University of Minnesota-Duluth where he won the Hobey Baker Award in 1984. Kurvers scored 45 points as a rookie and later contributed to six other clubs before retiring in 1995.

10   MIKE LALOR   BUFFALO, NEW YORK

As a rookie, Lalor helped Montreal win the Stanley Cup in 1985–86. Through the rest of the decade he was part of a defensive corps that was among the best in the NHL. Lalor moved on to play in St. Louis, Washington, Winnipeg, San Jose, and Dallas.

1

GARTH BOESCH

Regina Rangers, 1941

A member of the Regina Rangers for two years, Boesch won the Allan Cup in 1941 after playing three seasons with the Notre Dame Hounds in Saskatchewan junior hockey. He served a year in the military, and after a season with the Leafs' farm team in Pittsburgh played defence for Toronto from 1946 to 1950. He was the only NHLer of his era to sport a moustache.

Garth Boe

2

ART CHAPMAN

Port Arthur Seniors, 1925 and 1926

In 1924, Chapman played with the vaunted Winnipeg Falcons, the team that had developed into a world-class outfit and destroyed the competition at the 1920 Olympics in Antwerp. He won the Allan Cup both years with Port Arthur, and three years later began a 12-year NHL career with Boston and the New York Americans.

3

NEIL COLVILLE

Ottawa Commandos, 1943

Colville left the Rangers in 1942 to join the military, and it was while stationed in Ottawa that he won the Allan Cup. He also played with Winnipeg in the RCAF before rejoining the "Broadway Blueshirts" toward the end of the 1944–45 season.

4

WOODY DUMART

Ottawa RCAF, 1942

Dumart won the Allan Cup playing military hockey while on leave from the NHL. He missed three full seasons, but came back to play nine more with the Bruins, the only team he played for in his 16-year NHL career.

DOUG HARVEY

Montreal Royals, 1947

Harvey won the Allan Cup in his final year of pre-NHL hockey, the culmination of his time first with the Montreal Junior Royals (1942–45) in junior and then with the Royals (1945–47) in senior hockey.

JOE KLUKAY

Windsor Bulldogs, 1963

Another unique situation. Klukay won the Allan Cup *after* his NHL career was over. He retired from the Maple Leafs in 1956, having won four Stanley Cups with the Blue and White, but he was reinstated as an amateur and played most of 1956 to 1964 with the Windsor Bulldogs.

BERT McCAFFERY

Toronto Granites, 1922 and 1923

McCaffery played for the Granites, arguably one of the greatest amateur teams in Canada's history, from 1920 to 1924. The team went virtually undefeated for these two years, and at the 1924 Olympics destroyed the competition to win gold. McCaffery was one of only a few players who went on to play pro in the NHL and part of an even smaller group of players who won the Allan Cup, Olympic gold, and Stanley Cup.

GRANT WARWICK

Regina Rangers, 1941

Warwick made the leap from Allan Cup team to the NHL in one summer, joining the Rangers in the fall of 1941. After his NHL career was done, he and his brothers Bill and Dick represented Canada as members of the Penticton Vees at the 1955 World Championships and won gold. It was the only time three brothers played for Canada in international competition.

1 1990 OSHAWA 4 KITCHENER 3 (2OT)

Kitchener twice took a one-goal lead that was immediately answered by their opponent. Oshawa took a 3–2 lead in the third period only to have the Rangers' Gilbert Dionne respond. The first overtime period featured spectacular goaltending from the Rangers' Mike Torchia and Oshawa's Fred Brathwaite who had earlier replaced injured starter Kevin Butt. The Cup was won at 2:05 of the second overtime.

2 1989 SWIFT CURRENT 4 SASKATOON 3

The host Saskatoon Blades played the Swift Current Broncos in the 1989 Final — a rematch of the former's 5–4 upset win the round-robin stage. This was the first time two WHL clubs faced one another in junior hockey's biggest game. The Blades fought back from a 2–0 deficit and eventually took a 3–2 lead heading into the final period. Swift Current tied matters early in the third then won the championship in overtime.

3 1963 EDMONTON 4 NIAGARA FALLS 3

One of junior hockey's most storied franchises, the Edmonton Oil Kings won their first Memorial Cup at the expense of the Niagara Falls Flyers. In the sixth game of the best-of-seven final series, the Oil Kings led 4–0 before the Flyers staged a dramatic three-goal rally in the third period.

4 1992 KAMLOOPS 4 SAULT STE. MARIE 3

The Kamloops Blazers were the closest thing to a junior hockey dynasty with three Memorial Cup wins in four seasons between 1992 and 1995. In the first of these title victories the Blazers battled a strong Soo club from the OHL. The Greyhounds battled back from 3–0 and 4–3 deficits to tie the match in the final period. Kamloops stunned their opponent with only a few seconds left in the game.

5 **1958 REGINA 4   OTTAWA-HULL 3 (OT)**

These two junior affiliates of the Montreal Canadiens squared off in a championship series won by Ottawa-Hull in six games. Regina won game four in the most exciting match of the set. Top prospect Bill Hicke was instrumental in this win which got Regina back into the series. Ottawa had future Habs Jean-Claude Tremblay, Ralph Backstrom, Gilles Tremblay, and Bobby Rousseau on their roster.

6 **1946   WINNIPEG 4   ST. MIKE'S 2**

In one of the premier match-ups in Memorial Cup history, powerhouses of the east and west met to determine the nation's champion. The Winnipeg Monarchs defeated St. Mike's in a tough seven-game series in front of crowds in excess of 14,000 at Maple Leaf Gardens. Two third-period goals broke a 2–2 tie to bring the Cup to Manitoba. Future NHLer Harry Taylor starred for the Monarchs while St. Mike's had such notable figures as Tod Sloan and Fleming Mackell in their line-up.

7 **1988   MEDICINE HAT 7   WINDSOR 6**

The 1987–88 Windsor Spitfires were one of the best teams to lose a Memorial Cup Final. They dominated the OHL and were favoured to defeat the Medicine Hat Tigers in the championship game. Earlier in the tournament Windsor secured their place in the final match with an impressive 5–2 win over the Tigers. In a wild championship, Medicine Hat came back from a 3–0 deficit to forge ahead 6–4. Windsor tied it before the Tigers won the game with less than three minutes to play. Future NHLers Trevor Linden and Mark Fitzpatrick stood out for the champions.

8 **1977   NEW WESTMINSTER 6   OTTAWA 5**

The New Westminster Bruins won their first Memorial Cup with a thrilling victory in the final against the OHL's Ottawa 67's. The Bruins led by three goals entering the third period but the Ontario champions fought back to tie the match 5–5. Future NHL star Brad Maxwell scored the winner for the WHL champions.

9   1927   OWEN SOUND 5   PORT ARTHUR 4

Owen Sound swept Port Arthur in two straight games in the best-of-three final to claim the national title in 1927. The first match was a classic with Port Arthur matching the favoured Greys stride for stride. Future NHL players Red Beattie and Martin Lauder proved to be too much for Port Arthur. Lauder scored three times including the winner in the third period. The Greys wrapped up the title with a 5–3 win in the second match.

10   1936   WEST TORONTO 4   SASKATOON 2

Future Toronto Maple Leafs owner Harold Ballard managed West Toronto to a two-game sweep over Saskatoon in the 1936 championship. After winning the first game in relatively easy fashion, the Nationals were deadlocked with the Wesleys entering the third period. West Toronto eventually prevailed 4–2 but the Wesleys made quite an impression with their fast skating team.

Ron Ellis's **SEVEN KEY MOMENTS** From The **1972 CANADA-USSR** Summit Series

1

GAME 1   SEPTEMBER 2, 1972

USSR 7   Canada 3

Team Canada and its supporters expected to dominate the Soviets in the eight-game Summit Series. In the opening match at Montreal, Canada jumped to a 2–0 lead early in the first period. Gradually the superbly talented and well-conditioned USSR squad demonstrated their perserverance and waltzed to a 7–3 win. "The result jolted our team and sent shock waves through the whole country. Valeri Kharlamov killed us in that first game in one of the best individual performances I've ever seen," Ellis said.

2

GAME 3   SEPTEMBER 6, 1972

Canada 4   USSR 4

After evening the series in Game 2 by a 4–1 score, Canada let a 4–2 lead slip away and settled for a 4–4 tie in the third match played in Winnipeg. A key factor in this match was Soviet netminder Vladislav Tretiak, who faced 38 shots and was chosen the player-of-the-game for his team. "Had we won that game, after playing so well in Toronto, the momentum of two straight wins would have built our confidence considerably. Instead we let them back into the series and set the stage for our worst performance in Vancouver."

THE TRIP TO SWEDEN

After dropping two of the four games on their home rinks, Canada prepared for four matches that would take place in Moscow on the larger Olympic-sized ice surface. The team was still feeling from the disappointing results in Canada and the lack of fan support when it left to train in Sweden and play two exhibition matches against its national team. "Had we gone straight to Moscow after the horrible loss in Vancouver, I'd hate to think what might have happened. Instead we came together as a team in Sweden. We got used to the larger ice surface and put any personal differences from NHL rivalries aside once and for all. The two games in Sweden were rough and frustrating which helped galvanise our team spirit."

GAME 5   SEPTEMBER 22, 1972
USSR 5   Canada 4

This was the most heartbreaking game for Canadian fans to watch. A rejuvenated Team Canada took the play to their Soviet counterparts and built a 4–1 lead by the 4:56 mark of the third period. The USSR responded with four unanswered goals in less than six minutes. The victors hoped that this would break the Canadian spirit but that was not the case. "This was a pivotal game for our team. Despite the frustration, we proved that we could outplay them for a significant period of time. To a man, we felt confident that this was the last time we would lose a game in this series. The 3,000 Canadian supporters in the arena gave us a standing ovation after the loss which meant a great deal to us at this time."

GAME 6   SEPTEMBER 24, 1972
Canada 3   USSR 2

Canada embarked on its comeback trail by edging the USSR 3–2 in one of the better games of the series. Three goals in the first two minutes of the second period by Dennis Hull, Yvan Cournoyer, and Paul Henderson proved too much for the USSR to overcome. "Obviously we needed to win every game by this point in the series. We built on the confidence we gained from the previous game and started to shift the momentum in the series. I drew a penalty at 17:39 of the third period. Had they scored, a tie would have given them the series. Our guys killed off the penalty in what was probably the longest two minutes of my life."

GAME 8   SEPTEMBER 28, 1972
Canada 6   USSR 5

The third period of this match was one of the most memorable sequences of hockey in Canadian history. The USSR led 5–3 after the second period. Goals by Phil Esposito, Yvan Cournoyer, and Paul Henderson gave Canada a 6–5 win and the overall victory in the series. "That whole period was crucial. During the second intermission we were composed and confident. We knew we had to get a goal early and our top player Phil Esposito came through at the 2:27 mark. Cournoyer tied it with over seven minutes to play. This gave us plenty of time to get the goal we needed to claim outright victory in the series. Paul scored his third straight game-winning goal with 34 seconds left on the clock. It was a remarkable moment that will live on in Canadian history."

PAUL HENDERSON

Calling Pete Mahovlich off the ice in Game 8

A key sub-plot within the most famous game in Canadian hockey history was Paul Henderson's initiative during the last minute of the eighth game. With time running out, Henderson was on the Team Canada bench when he yelled at teammate Pete Mahovlich to change places with him. Mahovlich didn't hesitate and the rest is history. "You have to give Peter credit for hustling off. There was no time for second guessing at this late stage."

Ron Ellis and Vladislav Tretiak

Eight Best AMATEUR U.S. OLYMPIANS

1 ### PAT LAFONTAINE

Centre Lafontaine scored eight points in six games for Team USA at the 1984 Sarajevo Olympics then joined the New York Islanders at the end of the 1983–84 schedule. He recorded six 30-goal seasons on Long Island before he was traded to Buffalo where he finished second in the NHL scoring race with 148 points in 1992–93.

2 ### CHRIS CHELIOS

Chelios was with the U.S. Olympic Team in Sarajevo before playing a major part in the Montreal Canadiens' surprising run to the semifinals in 1983–84. He played for Team USA at the 1984 Canada Cup then won his first Norris Trophy in 1989. In 1990 Chelios was traded to Chicago. He also represented the U.S. at the 1987 and 1991 Canada Cups.

3 ### NEAL BROTEN

Broten was a key forward on the U.S. Olympic Team's stunning gold medal performance at the 1980 Lake Placid Olympics. He went on to a successful NHL career chiefly with the Minnesota North Stars. Broten also played for his country at the 1981 and 1984 Canada Cups along with the 1990 World Championships. In 1994–95 he scored 19 points in 20 playoff games for the Cup champion New Jersey Devils.

4 ### KEITH TKACHUK

In 1991–92 Tkachuk gained valuable experience playing for his country at the World Junior Championships and the Albertville Olympics. He registered consecutive 50-goal seasons for the Winnipeg Jets/Phoenix Coyotes franchise in 1995–96 and 1996–97, and he scored five goals in seven games while helping the U.S. win the inaugural World Cup of Hockey in 1996.

5 BRIAN LEETCH

Leetch played at the 1986 World Junior Championships, the 1987 Junior and Senior World Championships, and the 1988 Calgary Olympics. He joined New York late in 1987–88 and immediately fit in on their blueline. He scored 71 points the following season and won the Calder Trophy as the league's top rookie. In 1992 and 1997 Leetch was presented the James Norris Trophy and in 1994 he won the Conn Smythe.

6 DAVE CHRISTIAN

Right-winger Dave Christian scored eight points in seven games for the gold medal-winning U.S. team at the 1980 Lake Placid Olympics. His NHL career took him to Winnipeg, Washington, Boston, St. Louis, and Chicago. He retired in 1994 with 340 goals in 1,009 regular season games. Christian took part in the 1981, 1984, and 1991 Canada Cups as well as the 1981 and 1989 World Championships.

7 KEVIN STEVENS

Stevens excelled at Boston College before joining the U.S. National program the year of the Calgary Olympics. He recorded two 50-goal seasons and helped the Pittsburgh Penguins win consecutive Stanley Cups in 1991 and 1992. Stevens was chosen the left-winger on the NHL First All-Star team in 1992.

8 KEN MORROW

The 1980s were very good to Ken Morrow. He was a steady defenceman who made history in 1980 by winning a gold medal with the U.S. at the Lake Placid Olympics followed by a Stanley Cup with the New York Islanders. Morrow had plenty of time to savour the winning feeling as he played a part in the Islanders' four straight championships from 1980 to 1983. His presence on the blueline was an important component of New York's disciplined success over the years.

Ten WORST On-Ice ACCIDENTS

1

ACE BAILEY-EDDIE SHORE

In a game at the Boston Garden on December 12, 1933, Shore hit Bailey from behind, throwing him to the ice and knocking him unconscious. Red Horner of the Leafs then hit Shore with a force that knocked *him* out. Bailey needed multiple brain operations to save his life, and his career was over. Shore was suspended sixteen games and Horner six for their actions, and the following February a special All-Star game was held at Maple Leaf Gardens as a benefit for Bailey and his family.

2

BILL MASTERTON

Masterton was playing for the Minnesota North Stars against the California Seals in a game on January 13, 1968, when he collided with two players and hit his head on the ice. He lost consciousness, but when he came to, he tried to get up. He lapsed into a coma and died two days later, the day before the NHL All-Star game. It is the only on-ice fatality in the history of the NHL.

3

MARK HOWE

On December 29, 1980, while playing for the Hartford Whalers, Howe chased after a loose puck rolling toward his own goal. He lost his balance and crashed into the net, lifting it up a few inches and exposing a middle joint in the goal that acted like a sword. It pierced his buttock and narrowly missed his spinal column. He spent five weeks in the hospital and lost more than twenty pounds.

4

CLINT MALARCHUK

While playing goal for the Sabres in a game March 22, 1989, Malarchuk was crushed by two onrushing players — teammate Uwe Krupp and St. Louis's Steve Tuttle — and his throat was slashed by a skate in the process, opening a six-inch slice in his neck at his external jugular vein. He managed to skate off under his own steam while trainers pushed towels on the cut, and many fans were so disgusted and ill the Sabres' arena staff ran out of stretchers to administer first aid. Incredibly, Malarchuk returned later in the season.

GAYE STEWART–JIMMY ORLANDO

5 The Detroit-Toronto game of November 7, 1942, was ugly from the word go, and climaxed violently in an incident between Orlando and Stewart. They clashed behind referee Clancy's back, and as the pushing continued Clancy called Stewart for two minutes. Stewart came out of the penalty box, Orlando sucker-punched him, and Stewart cracked Orlando over the head with his stick, leaving the Wing dazed and semiconscious.

GORDIE HOWE–TED KENNEDY

6 Accounts vary about what happened in this playoff game, the first of the semifinals, on March 28, 1950. It is generally believed that Howe lost his balance while trying to hit Kennedy hard along the glass. Kennedy got out of the way and Howe fell head-first into the boards, losing consciousness. He suffered a fractured skull, broken nose, and scratched eyeball, and came close to death. He did not play again until the start of the next season.

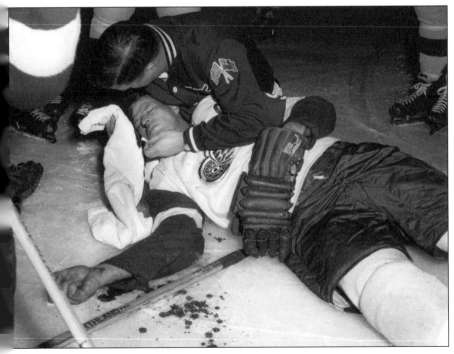

Gordie Howe

7 BRYAN MARCHMENT

In a playoff game April 18, 1997, in Dallas, Edmonton's Bryan Marchment shot the puck deep into the Stars' zone as he crossed centre ice. At the same moment, Guy Carbonneau came out of the penalty box near Marchment, who lost his balance on the shoot-in. Marchment fell backwards, head first into the corner of the boards where the penalty box door had opened. His helmet flew off as he fell, and his bare skull smashed against the corner of the door. He lost consciousness, and doctors had to stabilise his neck and insert tubes into his mouth before they could be sure he would be okay. He was carried off on a stretcher, but returned later in the series.

8 JOE WATSON

Watson's career came to an end November 10, 1978, while his Colorado Rockies were playing the St. Louis Blues. Skating back to get the puck along the boards on an icing, he was checked by Wayne Babych and crashed into the end of the rink. The bones in his right leg exploded into fourteen pieces, and his kneecap shattered in two places.

9 BERNIE PARENT

In February 1979, Parent was tending to his goal wearing his face-fitting fibreglass mask styled after Jacques Plante's. Defenceman Jim Watson was trying to tie up Rangers' rookie Don Maloney in front of the net, but Watson lost control of his stick, which poked Parent in the eye. Parent skated immediately to the bench in agony, ripping his mask off and covering his eyes with his hands. He was taken to Wills Eye Hospital in Philadelphia. Though his sight was saved, his career was over.

10 MICHEL GOULET

Goulet had a Hall of Fame career that spanned 1,089 games and 548 goals, but his career ended in disaster after he lost his balance following through on a slapshot while playing with Chicago on March 16, 1994. He slid head-first into the end boards and lost consciousness, only his thin, nonstandard helmet protecting his head. He was taken off the ice on a stretcher, and although he recovered fully from the injuries, his career was over. A year to the day later, the Quebec Nordiques, for whom he had played 11 of his 16 seasons, retired his number 16 at the Colisée.

Most Points By A **PLAYER** In His **ONLY** NHL **SEASON** (Since 1967)

48   MILAN NOVY

Novy had an outstanding career in Czechoslovakia in the late 1970s and early '80s. He was drafted by Washington in 1982 and played for the Caps as a 31-year-old rookie in 1982–83. He had an outstanding year, with 18 goals and 48 points, but returned to his native country the following season and never played again in the NHL.

37   BOB SULLIVAN

Drafted by the Rangers in 1977, Sullivan played five years in the IHL and AHL before signing with Hartford as a free agent for the '82–'83 season. He played part of the year with the farm team in Binghamton, but while with the NHL Whalers had 18 goals and 37 points. He failed to crack the lineup the following season.

36   ED HOEKSTRA

Hoekstra started his pro career in Original Six times but could never make the grade in the NHL. He played nine years of minor pro before the Flyers signed him for the team's first year, in '67–'68. He played 70 games for Philadelphia and had 15 goals, but the next year was back in the minors.

34   VLADIMIR KRUTOV

Krutov had a long and distinguished career in the Iron Curtain Soviet Union and did not make it to the NHL until he was nearly 30. He played just one season with the Vancouver Canucks, in 1989–90, and then retired, having played 61 NHL games and scoring eleven goals.

22   ULF ISAKSSON

Isaksson began his career in Sweden, but when Los Angeles drafted him in 1982 he came to North America to try his NHL luck. He made the team his first camp and had a respectable 22 points his rookie season, but the following year he returned to Sweden and never played again in the NHL.

STEVE CARLSON

21 Another player whose NHL debut was years in the making, Carlson played six seasons in the minors and then the WHA before Los Angeles gave him an NHL chance in 1982–83. In 52 games with the Kings he had 21 points, but the Kings gave up on him. In subsequent years, both Minnesota and Pittsburgh signed him, only to send him to their minor league teams.

ANTERO LEHTONEN

21 A Finnish league player, Lehtonen was never drafted and signed with Washington for '79–'80. He played 65 games for the Caps that year, but the trial was short-lived and the next year he was back in his homeland playing for Turku.

DAVID SAUNDERS

20 Another obscure name in the modern lexicon of the NHL player register, Saunders played with the Canucks in 1987–88 after being drafted by the team three seasons earlier. He played 56 games that year, but never made it back to the NHL.

TODD BERGEN

16 Bergen's path to the NHL was normal, though brief. He played for the Flyers after being drafted by the team, and in just 14 games had eleven goals and five assists. However, he played most of the year with Hershey in the AHL, and despite averaging more than a point a game, the only player on this list to do so. He never returned to the NHL.

Most Wins By A **GOALIE** In His **ONLY** NHL **SEASON**

10

HARVEY BENNETT

Although Bennett played professional hockey for almost 20 years, his NHL career started and ended in one season, 1944–45, with Boston. He appeared in 25 games and had a 10–12–2 record, and like many a wartime goalie he was deemed unneeded once regular Frank Brimsek returned from military service.

10

HEC HIGHTON

Another war replacement goalie, Highton played '43–'44 with Chicago with a 10–14–0 record as a 20-year-old. However, the Hawks didn't consider him enough of a prospect, and Highton finished his career in the minors.

10

HERB RHEAUME

Rheaume played for the Canadiens during one of the worst seasons in franchise history, 1925–26, when the team failed to make the playoffs. In 31 games he was 10–20–1, and he spent the next ten years in the minor pro leagues, never to return to the NHL.

9

DON HEAD

Head was 28 before he played his first NHL game, with Boston, in 1961–62. He had a miserable 9–26–3 record, and as a result spent the next ten years in the WHL.

8

JIM CORSI

Undrafted, Corsi began his career in the WHA before signing on with the Edmonton Oilers just before their first NHL season in 1979–80. He played only 26 games, with an 8–14–3 record, but spent most of the year in the minors before moving to Italy, where he had a long and successful career.

SETH MARTIN

8 Martin was, in his day, the most famous Canadian athlete in Europe, thanks to his continuous participation at the amateur level in the World Championships. He played more games in goal than any other Canadian national goaler, but played just 30 games in the NHL, with the expansion St. Louis Blues, in '67–'68, where he teamed with Glenn Hall to take the Blues to the Stanley Cup finals.

LARRY LOZINSKI

6 Lozinski was drafted by Detroit in 1978, and two years later played his first league game with the Red Wings, though he spent much of the season in the minors. In 30 games, he had a 6–11–7 record but never made it with the club the next season or any other.

JIM McLEOD

6 An almost 20-year career saw McLeod in the NHL for just 16 games, during which time he had a 6–6–4 record with the 1971–72 Blues in St. Louis as a 34-year-old rookie. He played in the WHA for three years before retiring at age 38.

Seth Martin in goa

Most **POINTS** By A Player In His **FINAL** **YEAR** In The NHL (pre-1967)

53 **SYL APPS**
"Slippery Syl" to some, "the Commish" to others, captain Apps finished his career on the highest possible note, scoring a hat trick in his final game, the 199th, 200th, and 201st goals of his distinguished career. He played ten years in the league, interrupted by two years of military service, and was among the first men elected to the Hockey Hall of Fame, in 1961.

50 **GORD DRILLON**
Drillon played just 311 games in seven NHL seasons, and his 50-point final season with Montreal was almost as good as his best season with the Leafs, when he scored 52 points to lead the NHL in 1937–38.

48 **GERRY HEFFERNAN**
Heffernan played only two full seasons in the league, a wartime replacement on a strong Canadiens team. In 1943–44, he scored 48 points (28 goals) in 43 games with the team, but spent most of his career with the Montreal Royals of the old Quebec Senior league.

44 **BUZZ BOLL**
Boll's best two point-production years of his 12-year career were his last two, with the Boston Bruins. In 1942–43 he had 52 points, and his last NHL season he had 44, far better than his highest totals with the Leafs or the Americans, with whom he played before coming to Beantown.

41 **TOM ANDERSON**
Anderson played only seven seasons in the NHL, one with Detroit and the rest with the Americans in New York. His last year, 1941–42, was one point better than his previous best of 40 three years earlier.

40 RED SULLIVAN

Sullivan played for Boston, Chicago, and New York over eleven years and did not miss a game in his last four NHL seasons. After retiring from the Rangers, he was the team's coach for almost two years.

38 BILL COWLEY

One of the game's greats, Cowley also took the high road by retiring before his skills had diminished. A Hall of Famer, he played a dozen seasons with the Bruins after a rookie year with the St. Louis Eagles. Thirteen of his 195 career goals came in his final season, 1946–47.

38 RED KELLY

One of the greatest players ever to skate in the NHL, Kelly retired in 1967 at the age of 40. His final year, which included a Stanley Cup with Toronto, allowed him to go out on top after eight Cups and some 1,300 games. He had 823 career points, 38 of which came in his last season.

36 BUDDY O'CONNOR

Another Hall of Famer, O'Connor split his NHL time between the Rangers and Habs, finishing with the Broadway Blueshirts in '50–'51. He scored 16 goals in his final year, his third-best season.

36 BERT OLMSTEAD

A reclamation project by coach Punch Imlach in Toronto, Olmstead served as assistant coach during most of his four years with the Leafs, 1958–62. His 36 points in '61–'62 pushed his career total to 602 and made him one of the highest-scoring players of the Original Six.

FEWEST Career NHL GOALS After A 50-GOAL Season

1 BOBBY HULL   6

Immediately after registering his fifth 50-goal season in 1971–72, Chicago Blackhawks superstar Bobby Hull shocked the hockey world by signing with the Winnipeg Jets of the newly founded WHA. He topped the 50-goal mark four times in seven years, including a career best 77 in 1974–75 while playing on an explosive line with Swedes Anders Hedberg and Ulf Nilsson. Hull rejoined the NHL with the Winnipeg Jets and Hartford Whalers in 1979–80, where he scored his last six NHL goals.

2 JACQUES RICHARD   24

Left-winger Jacques Richard demonstrated his immense offensive gift for one season when he scored 52 goals for the Quebec Nordiques in 1980–81. But in 1981–82 he failed to sustain his production and dropped off to 15 goals. The next year Richard scored only nine times and was eventually sent down to Fredericton of the AHL. He retired that summer with 160 career goals in 556 regular-season games.

3 MICKEY REDMOND   26

Right-winger Mickey Redmond began his NHL tenure with the Montreal Canadiens where he won a Stanley Cup in 1968–69. He went to the Detroit Red Wings in 1970–71 and had 42 goals in his first full year with the Wings before scoring 52 and 51 goals in 1972–73 and 1973–74. A chronic back injury limited him to 26 goals in 66 regular season games after those three stellar years.

4 HAKAN LOOB   27

Swedish right-winger Hakan Loob played six NHL seasons for the Calgary Flames. He recorded at least 30 goals four times, including 50 in 1987–88. Loob followed up by scoring 27 times in 1988–89 and helping the Flames win their first-ever Stanley Cup before returning to Sweden in 1989–90.

Grant joined the Minnesota North Stars prior to the 1968–69 season. He scored 34 times that year and was named the Calder Trophy winner. Grant scored 176 goals in six years with the North Stars then was sent to the Detroit Red Wings for Henry Boucha. In 1974–75 Grant hit the 50-goal mark for the first time. Over the next five years in Detroit and Los Angeles he was unable to play a full season because of injuries and could only muster 34 goals in 170 games.

Danny Grant

6   MIKE BOSSY   38

One of hockey's most prolific goal scorers, New York Islanders' right-winger Mike Bossy scored at least 50 goals in each of his first nine NHL seasons. He hit the 60-goal plateau five times and helped the Islanders win four straight Stanley Cups from 1980 to 1983. Back trouble limited him to 38 goals in 63 games in 1986–87 and he was forced to retire at the end of that year.

7   GARY LEEMAN   47

Although he played defence in junior, Leeman found his NHL niche as a forward. He spent most of his career with the Toronto Maple Leafs where he topped the 20-goal mark four straight years from 1986–87 to 1989–90. In the last of these seasons Leeman scored 51 times. He never regained his touch after that big year. A change of scenery in Calgary, Montreal, Vancouver, and St. Louis resulted in only 47 goals in his final 122 games.

8   CAM NEELY   53

Neely was traded from Vancouver to Boston in June 1986. He registered three 50-goal seasons and helped the Beantowners reach the Stanley Cup finals in 1988 and 1990. Neely hit the 50-goal mark for the last time in 1993–94 even though he appeared in only 49 games. A degenerative hip condition caused his production to drop to 53 goals over his last two NHL seasons, and he retired in 1996 with 395 career scores.

9   KEN HODGE   71

Hodge was enjoying a respectable start to his NHL career when he was sent to Boston in May 1967. He topped the 40-goal mark three times including a personal high of 50 in 1973–74. After that year Hodge cooled off and was eventually traded to the New York Rangers.

10   BLAINE STOUGHTON   73

Stoughton was a decent NHL forward from 1973 to 1976 when he scored 34 goals in 155 games for Pittsburgh and Toronto. In 1979–80 he rejoined the NHL with Hartford and tied for the NHL lead with 56 goals. Two years later registered 52 then in 1982–83 he tallied 45 times but played only one more season after that.

Ten **FORGOTTEN FACTS** About The
1994 **OWNERS' LOCKOUT**

1

THE ROSTER
for the Touring "Ninety-Nine All-Stars"

Goal: Grant Fuhr, Kelly Hrudey

Defence: Rob Blake, Paul Coffey, Todd Gill, Charlie Huddy, Al MacInnis, Marty McSorley

Forward: Wayne Gretzky, Pat Conacher, Russ Courtnall, Sergei Fedorov, Tony Granato, Brett Hull, Steve Larmer, Kirk Muller, Mark Messier, Rick Tocchet, Steve Yzerman

Coach: Doug Wilson / Assistant: Walter Gretzky

2

THE UNIFORM DESIGN
Based on the 1920s Detroit jersey with "Ninety-Nine" replacing "Detroit" on the crest and the NHLPA logo added to the upper left.

3

GILMOUR IN SWITZERLAND
As a result of the lockout, Toronto captain Doug Gilmour opted to play in Switzerland for a short time to keep in shape. He joined Rapperswil, a First Division team, for 12 games in late November and early December, scoring twice with 15 assists before joining the Gretzky All-Stars.

4

COPPS COLISEUM TOURNAMENT
Other NHL players joined up in Hamilton and played an exhibition tournament for charity. The games were played November 10–12, 1994, at Copps Coliseum, and featured four teams — Ontario, Quebec, Western Canada, and the United States — and drew near-capacity crowds in the 17,000-seat arena.

5

NHL DRAWS
up 48-game season-saving schedule

The schedule was reduced to just 48 games, the same length as the 1941–42 season. New Jersey won the Cup after compiling a regular season record of 22–18–8, the worst for a Cup winner since the '48–'49 Leafs won after a fourth-place record of 22–25–13.

6

THE RESULTS

of the "Ninety-Nine All-Stars" Tour

December 1, 1994 vs. Detroit Vipers (4–3 loss)

December 3, 1994 vs. Jokerit (Finland — 7–1 win)

December 4, 1994 vs. Ilves Tampere (Finland — 4–3 OT loss)

December 6, 1994 vs. Norwegian Spectrum All-Stars (6–3 win)

December 9, 1994 vs. Djurgarden (Sweden — 9–3 win)

December 10, 1994 vs. Vastra Frolunda (Sweden — 5–2 win)

December 12, 1994 vs. Malmo (Sweden — 6–5 OT loss)

December 14, 1994 vs. German All-Stars (8–5 win)

7

PLAYER EXECUTIVES

The NHLPA president was Mike Gartner, and during negotiations there were four vice-presidents: Ken Baumgartner, Andy Moog, Kelly Miller, and Guy Carbonneau.

8

NO ALL-STAR GAME

The All-Star game, set for San Jose in January, was cancelled, the first time in league history this happened.

9

THE THREAT

During the heat of the lockout, Chris Chelios uttered a threat at NHL Commissioner Gary Bettman via the media: "If I was Gary Bettman, I'd be worried about my family, my well-being, right now." Mathieu Schneider of Montreal taped a message on his helmet, which read: "Bettman Sucks."

10

HANDSHAKES

At the end of each preseason game, players exchanged "solidarity handshakes" to indicate their unified support for the NHLPA.

Ten **WORST RETURNS** For A **TRADED MARQUEE** Player

1   **BOSTON — COONEY WEILAND**

Boston centre Cooney Weiland was an offensive star who led the NHL in scoring with 73 points in 44 games in 1929–30. He formed the well known "Dynamite Line" with Dutch Gainor and Dit Clapper and helped Boston win its first Stanley Cup in 1929. Weiland was sent to the Ottawa Senators prior to the 1932–33 season for Joe Lamb and cash. While the money involved was substantial, Lamb was a decent right-winger who played 443 NHL games. Weiland, in contrast, was elected to the Hockey Hall of Fame in 1971.

2   **DETROIT — TED LINDSAY**

Left-winger Ted Lindsay was one of the greatest players in the history of the Detroit franchise. He was an eight-time selection to the NHL First All-Star Team and was the winner of the Art Ross Trophy in 1950. Following the 1956–57 season he was sent to Chicago with Glenn Hall and Forbes Kennedy for Hank Bassen, Johnny Wilson, and Bill Preston. Wilson was a durable left-winger, Bassen a journeyman netminder, and Preston never played in the NHL.

3   **DETROIT — RED KELLY**

Kelly was one of the NHL's top defencemen in the 1950s and a key component in four Detroit Stanley Cup wins. He won the first ever James Norris Trophy in 1954 and was also a four-time winner of the Lady Byng Trophy. He was sent by the Wings to Toronto during the 1959–60 season for defenceman Marc Reaume. The Maple Leafs converted Kelly to forward and made him an important part of the team that won four Stanley Cups between 1962 and 1967. He was elected to the Hockey Hall of Fame in 1969. Reaume was a steady blueliner who played 344 NHL games but was not in the same class as Kelly.

4   **TORONTO — TIM HORTON**

Horton was a rock on the Toronto Maple Leafs' defence for nearly two decades. He formed an outstanding partnership with Allan Stanley and was a key reason why Toronto won four Stanley

Cups in the 1960s. He was traded to the New York Rangers on March 3, 1970, for future considerations that ended up being Denis Dupere. Horton continued to provide experience and stability in New York, Pittsburgh, and Buffalo before his tragic death in 1974. He was elected to the Hockey Hall of Fame in 1977. Dupere was a utility player for parts of four seasons with Toronto and retired with 80 career goals in 421 regular season games.

5 DETROIT — MARCEL DIONNE

Dionne was coming off a 121-point season with Detroit when he signed with the Los Angeles Kings. The resulting dispute was settled by a trade in which Dan Maloney and Terry Harper were exchanged for Dionne. Both Maloney and Harper were solid players who enjoyed twelve- and nineteen-year careers respectively. Dionne topped the 100-point mark seven times for the Kings and retired with 1,771 points. He was elected to the Hockey Hall of Fame in 1992.

6 TORONTO — DARRYL SITTLER

The Toronto Maple Leafs traded their all-time leading scorer to the Philadelphia Flyers on January 20, 1982. In return they received collegiate star Rich Costello, a second-round draft pick that was used to claim Peter Ihnacak, and future considerations which turned out to be Ken Strong. Sittler scored 84 goals in 191 games for the Flyers before he was traded to Detroit prior to the 1984–85 season. Costello and Strong played 12 and 15 games respectively. Ihnacak was a decent role player for Toronto with 267 points in 417 career games.

7 WASHINGTON — DENNIS MARUK

Maruk was a consistent offensive threat throughout his career who was at his best with the Washington Capitals. In 343 regular season contests for the club he scored 182 goals and 431 points. Washington traded him to Minnesota for a second-round draft pick which turned out to be journeyman right-winger Stephen Leach who scored 274 career points. Maruk totalled 878 points in 888 career games and represented Canada at four World Championships.

Marcel Dionne

QUEBEC — MICHEL GOULET

8 Goulet was the most prolific goal scorer in the history of the Quebec Nordiques. Between 1982 and 1986 he reached the 50-goal mark four straight seasons. On March 5, 1990, he was sent to Chicago along with Greg Millen for Dan Vincelette, Mario Doyon, and Everett Sanipass. Goulet scored 92 goals in a Chicago uniform and helped the team reach the Stanley Cup finals in 1992. He was elected to the Hockey Hall of Fame 1998. The three players exchanged for him combined to play only 77 games with the Nordiques.

QUEBEC — PETER STASTNY

9 Stastny was a key figure when the Quebec Nordiques reached the Stanley Cup semifinals in 1982 and 1985. Between 1980–81 and 1985–86 he recorded six consecutive 100-point seasons. On March 6, 1990, he was traded to the New Jersey Devils for Craig Wolanin and future considerations (Randy Velischek). Even though Stastny's best years were behind him, he scored 173 points for New Jersey in 217 regular season games. Wolanin and Velischek were but solid role players.

WASHINGTON — DINO CICCARELLI

10 Right-winger Dino Ciccarelli was one of the top goal scorers in the NHL in the 1980s and 1990s. To acquire him and Bob Rouse the Capitals sent Mike Gartner and Larry Murphy to Minnesota. When the Capitals moved Ciccarelli in June 1992, they received Kevin Miller. Ciccarelli continued to score well in Motown and helped the team reach the Stanley Cup finals in 1995. Miller played only ten games for Washington in 1992–93 before he was sent to St. Louis for defenceman Paul Cavallini.

1 DOUG HARVEY — ST. LOUIS

A key member of Montreal's five-Cup run from 1956–60, Harvey played 14 seasons with the Habs before becoming playing-coach of the Rangers in 1961. He stayed on Broadway for three years, then played two games with Detroit in 1966–67. His last stop was St. Louis, where he joined Hall and Plante for the '68–'69 season before hangin' 'em up for good at the age of 44.

2 FLASH HOLLETT — N.Y. AMERICANS

Hollett began his career in 1933 with the Leafs and Ottawa Senators, but he was known mostly as a Boston Bruin, for whom he played almost nine seasons. Midway through the '43–'44 season he was traded to Detroit for Pat Egan, playing two and a half seasons with the Winged Wheel before retiring. In '44–'45, he accomplished a remarkable feat for a defenceman, scoring 20 goals in a 50-game season.

3 BOBBY HULL — HARTFORD

Hull's 15-year career with the Blackhawks will never be forgotten, nor will his spectacular departure from the NHL to the Winnipeg Jets of the WHA. When the Jets became part of the new NHL in 1979–80, Hull was still with the team. But not many people remember that during the season he was traded to the Hartford Whalers for future considerations, and for nine games played with two other greats, Gordie Howe and Dave Keon.

4 ANDY MOOG — MONTREAL

Moog was an integral part of the Oilers dynasty for seven seasons (1980–87) before being traded to Boston and then Dallas. But at the end of his 17-year career, he signed as a free agent with Montreal, and for one year tried to resuscitate the Habs' flagging reputation. He had an 18–17–5 record with Montreal, but could not get the team past the second round of the playoffs. At season's end, he retired.

5 ### BOBBY ORR — CHICAGO

Perhaps the most famous of all free agents in the modern sports world, Orr left his hallowed Bruins in 1976 to sign with Chicago on the advice of his agent, Alan Eagleson. Orr played just 20 games his first year with the Hawks, then took a season off to rest his battered knees before trying one more time to regain his old form. Six games into the '78–'79 season, he knew he was no longer the star of his glory years and retired.

6 ### PIERRE PILOTE — TORONTO

Pilote played 13 Original Six seasons (eight times not missing a single game) with the Blackhawks before being traded in the off-season of 1968 to the Leafs for Jim Pappin. After one disappointing year with the Leafs when the team did not make the playoffs, he retired.

7 ### JACQUES PLANTE — BOSTON

Plante just kept playing and playing and playing. After 11 remarkable seasons with the Habs, including six Stanley Cups and six Vezina Trophies, Jake the Snake joined the Rangers for two seasons, the Blues and Glenn Hall for two more, and the Leafs for three. But his last NHL team, some 20 years after his pro debut, was the Boston Bruins, who had acquired him from the Leafs with a third-round draft choice (Doug Gibson) for a first-round draft choice (Ian Turnbull) and future considerations (Ed Johnston). Plante played eight games with Boston, with a great 7–1 record, before joining the WHA Edmonton Oilers two years later.

8 ### LARRY ROBINSON — LOS ANGELES

Robinson began his career with the Montreal Canadiens in 1972–73 and was a mainstay on the blueline through four Stanley Cups at decade's end. But in 1989, after 17 years and 1,100 games, he signed with the west coast Kings, where he played three years. A further three years later, he was the team's coach.

9 · BORJE SALMING — DETROIT

One of the first truly European-trained players to make it to the NHL, Salming was signed by the Leafs in the summer of 1973. He played more than 1,000 games with Toronto over a fantastic 16-year career, but in 1989 he signed as a free agent with the Red Wings, where he played the final year of his NHL career.

10 · STEVE SMITH — CALGARY

Smith's career can be neatly divided into two eras, his seven years with the Oilers during the dynastic 1980s, and his six years with the Blackhawks in the early '90s. But the 1998–99 season was considered by many in Alberta an ugly anomaly as Smith played for the Oilers' dreaded enemy, the Calgary Flames.

Last Ten **PLAYERS** From The **ORIGINAL SIX** Era

1

WAYNE CASHMAN 1964-83

Cashman combined hard-nosed play with an ability to produce offensively during a career spent entirely with the Boston Bruins. He recorded eight 20-goal seasons and was chosen to represent Canada in the Summit Series in 1972. Both he and Carol Vadnais remained from the Original Six period in 1982–83 but Cashman's career was prolonged because of the Bruins' run to the Stanley Cup semifinals.

2

CAROL VADNAIS 1966-83

Vadnais began his career in the Montreal Canadiens' organization but gained his first chance to play regularly in the NHL with the Oakland Seals in 1968–69. He spent nearly four seasons in the Golden State before a trade brought him to Boston in time for their run to the Stanley Cup title in 1971–72. Vadnais spent seven years with the New York Rangers then played his last 51 games with New Jersey in 1982–83.

3

DON MARCOTTE 1965-82

Marcotte was a well rounded left-winger who played every one of his 868 NHL regular season games with the Boston Bruins. A one-game appearance in 1965–66 was his only taste of the NHL in the Original Six era. Marcotte totalled 230 goals and 484 points and played with the Bruins until the second round of the 1982 playoffs.

4

ROGIE VACHON 1966-82

Vachon emerged with the Montreal Canadiens in 1966–67. He led all netminders with six playoff wins when the Habs reached the last Original Six Stanley Cup Final and helped the Habs win the Cup in 1968 and 1969. Vachon enjoyed his greatest workload with the Los Angeles Kings where he was the first-string goalie for seven years. He also played with Detroit and Boston before retiring in 1981–82 after the Bruins were eliminated by Quebec in the second round of the playoffs.

DAVE KEON 1960-82

5

Keon joined the Toronto Maple Leafs in 1960–61 when he scored 45 points and won the Calder Trophy. Keon played a key role in four Maple Leafs Stanley Cup wins in the 1960s and in 1967 won the Conn Smythe Trophy. He also played three seasons with the Hartford Whalers from 1979 to 1982.

ROSS LONSBERRY 1966-81

6

Lonsberry's tenure in the Original Six period consisted of eight games with the Boston Bruins in 1966–67. He moved on to the Los Angeles Kings where he recorded consecutive 20-goal seasons in 1969–70 and 1970–71. Lonsberry then played for the Philadelphia Flyers where he contributed to two Stanley Cup championships. He played his last three years in Pittsburgh where his final five games came in the first round of the 1980–81 playoffs.

Dave Keon

7 JEAN RATELLE 1960-81

Ratelle began with the New York Rangers where he helped the club reach the Stanley Cup finals in 1972 when he centred the potent "Goal-A-Game (GAG)" line with Rod Gilbert and Vic Hadfield. That year he won the Lester B. Pearson Award and the Lady Byng Trophy. He was traded to Boston where he won his second Lady Byng Award in 1976 and helped the Bruins reach the finals in 1977 and 1978. He retired after Boston was swept in the first round of the 1981 playoffs by the Minnesota North Stars.

8 AL SMITH 1965-81

Goalie Al Smith played three games with the Toronto Maple Leafs in 1965–66 and 1966–67. He became the first-string netminder with Pittsburgh and Detroit then played for Buffalo and Hartford. His last NHL games were the 37 regular season contests he played for the Colorado Rockies in 1980–81.

9 TERRY HARPER 1962-81

Defenceman Terry Harper began with the Montreal Canadiens in 1962–63 and won five Stanley Cups with the Habs before joining Los Angeles in 1972–73. Prior to the 1975–76 campaign he was sent to Detroit. Harper played one year in St. Louis and Colorado before retiring at the end of the 1980–81 regular season. Along the way he recorded 256 career points and took part in four All-Star Games.

10 RON ELLIS 1964-81

In 1964 Ellis embarked on a successful NHL career spent entirely with the Maple Leafs. Though Ellis was lauded for his checking ability, he set a team record with ten straight 20-goal seasons from 1966–75. He won a Stanley Cup in 1967 and played for Canada during the 1972 Summit Series. Ellis returned to play for Canada at the 1977 World Championships then played four and a half seasons with Toronto. He retired part way through the 1980–81 season with 332 goals in 1,034 regular season games.

Twelve **"B" PLAYERS** From The Original Six **BORN** In **WINNIPEG**

1

DOUG BALDWIN

Baldwin played just 24 NHL games in a 20-year hockey career that began with the Winnipeg Rangers of the MJHL and finished with the Washington Presidents of the EHL. In his short time in the bigs, he played for Toronto, Detroit, and Chicago, and recorded one assist.

2

FRANK BATHGATE

Bathgate was in the line-up for only two NHL games, with the Rangers in '52–'53, as a 32-year-old. He played most of the season with Shawinigan of the Quebec Senior league, and finished in OHA Senior league play, retiring in 1962.

3

BILL BENSON

Born July 29, 1920, Bill Benson played half a season with the New York Americans in '40–'41. The next year the team transferred to Brooklyn for one final year before folding. He missed 1943–45 while serving in the military and never returned to the NHL, playing the final five years of his pro career in the AHL.

4

BOBBY BENSON

This Benson, unrelated to Bill, was part of Canada's first Olympic hockey team, the 1920 Winnipeg Falcons, that waltzed to a gold medal in Antwerp. He played but briefly in the NHL, eight games with Boston in '24–'25, having little desire to make a career as a pro.

5

ANDY BLAIR

The only NHLer of his era to sport a moustache, Blair had a significant and successful career. He played nine years and 402 games in the NHL, eight of those seasons with the Leafs, and won the Stanley Cup the team's first year at Maple Leaf Gardens, 1931–32.

HELGE BOSTROM

6   The only NHLer named Helge, Bostrom played 96 games on defence over four NHL seasons with Chicago from 1929–33, making his debut at the advanced age of 35. He scored three goals and three assists during his career, and in 13 playoff games never scored a point.

RALPH BOWMAN

7   Bowman began his fine career with the Ottawa Senators and the St. Louis Eagles before settling in with the Red Wings midway through the '34–'35 season. He won two Stanley Cups with Detroit, and was a steady and reliable defenceman who never scored much (eight goals in 274 career games). His arrival in Detroit was the result of one of the biggest trades of his generation, the Eagles sending Bowman and Syd Howe to the Motor City for Ted Graham and $50,000.

Andy Blair

8   JACK BOWNASS

Another career minor leaguer, Bownass played four seasons with the Rangers and Canadiens, scoring three goals in 80 regular-season games (he never took part in the playoffs). He finished his career as a member of Canada's national teams in the mid-1960s after being reinstated as an amateur.

9   ANDY BRANIGAN

Branigan made his NHL debut as an 18-year-old with the Americans in 1940, but after just six games was sent to the Springfield Indians of the AHL where he finished the season. The next fall, he stayed in New York for 21 games, but again was sent to the Indians and was never heard of again in NHL circles. He played professionally for another 19 years, mostly in the American League.

10   GEORGE BROWN

Brown played a total of 79 games over three seasons with the Canadiens in the late 1930s. Although his rights were at one time owned also by the Maroons, Rangers, and Boston, the Habs were the only team to give him a chance in the NHL, though he never came close to any playoff glory with the *bleu, blanc, et rouge* before leaving the game.

11   AL BUCHANAN

Buchanan played three games for the Leafs in '48–'49 and one game the next year, but that was the only NHL action he ever saw. He wound up in OHA Senior play and retired in 1955 after finishing the season with the Niagara Falls Cataracts.

12   BILL BUREGA

Burega played hockey for some 21 years, starting with the MJHL, going to the Western League and finishing in the OHA Senior loop. He played only four NHL games, with the Leafs in 1955–56, and earned one assist, but he spent most of the season with the Winnipeg Warriors of the WHL.

STANDARDISED ICE SIZE

1 Before 1929, NHL rinks could range from 112' by 58' to 250' by 116'. The league specified the rink size as 200' by 85' for the 1929–30 season. Over the years teams such as Boston and Chicago were allowed to play on slightly smaller surfaces, but the standard was set.

VISIBLE TIME CLOCK

2 By the 1933–34 season each NHL arena was required to have a time clock visible to fans and players. Before this the only time clock in the building was that used by the official timekeeper at ice surface level. Four-sided electrical clocks got the fans in attendance more into the game and could influence the strategy of a coach.

CREATION OF THE GOAL CREASE

3 An L-shaped area painted at the front of the net was made mandatory prior to the 1934–35 season as a means of protecting NHL netminders. Opposing forwards and defencemen would no longer be allowed to station themselves on top of the goalie or crash the net during a rush. The goal crease served as protection for goal-keepers and forced teams to be more innovative in their offensive strategy.

THE ICING RULE

4 The NHL introduced the icing rule in time for the start of the 1937–38 season. It was intended to deter teams with the lead from dumping the puck down the length of the ice to preserve their advantage. The icing rule sped up the game and rewarded offensive teams by granting them a face-off in their opponent's zone.

THE RED LINE AND FORWARD PASSING

5 In 1943–44 the common markings of the present-day NHL rink were completed when the centre-ice red line was added. The red line created a neutral zone at centre ice and forward passing from one zone to another was introduced. Today's icing calls and two-line off-side passes are oriented around this line.

6 ICE RESURFACING

Prior to the 1940–41 season the NHL established the cleaning of the ice surface between periods. The improved ice conditions sped up the game and eliminated many of the dangerous cracks that often formed. By the next decade, Frank Zamboni's driver-operated resurfacing vehicle was being used at the Montreal Forum. Zamboni machines could be found in each of the six NHL arenas by the early 1960s.

7 SAFETY HEEL FOR SKATES

In the early 1960s CCM developed a plastic guard intended to cover the heel of players' skates. Many skaters had been cut or dangerously entangled during games over the years. Before the 1964–65 season started, the NHL required all players to wear the new form of protection.

8 RESHAPING THE NET

Following an horrific injury to Mark Howe in 1984–85, the net was restructured to eliminate the sharp metal point along the middle of its base. The back of the net was flattened so that nothing dangerous was pointing out in the event a player was pushed into the goal area. The pegs holding the net in place were altered so the net would give way to heavy contact, so that injuries would be less likely.

9 MANDATORY USE OF A HELMET

There was a time when helmets were considered a nuisance by players but the increased size of players and the faster pace of the game created a greater need for head protection. The first motion passed by the NHL required all players who signed contracts after June 1, 1979, to wear helmets. An exemption was made to players in 1992–93 provided they signed a legal waiver, but in practice helmets have become a standard piece of equipment.

Ten Long-**FORGOTTEN REGULATIONS**
From The **1931-32** Rule Book

1 "Should any accidents occur after all the players named shall have participated in a match, and there is not a full team of six players available, the opposing club must drop sufficient players to equalize."

2 "The puck may be passed forward by any player to a player of the same side in any one of the three zones into which the ice is divided, but may not be passed forward from a player in one zone to a player of the same side in another zone."

3 "Not more than three players (including the goal-keeper) of the defending side may be in their defending zone when the puck is in any other zone. Should a team violate this rule, it shall incur a minor penalty for each infraction."

4 "A player beyond his defence area shall not pass or carry the puck backward into his defence area for the purpose of delaying the game. The penalty for infraction of this rule shall be a minor penalty to the offending player."

5 "No goal-keeper shall be permitted to hold the puck with his hands or arms. He may catch the puck in his hand but must clear immediately and must not throw the puck forward towards his opponents' goal. For infringement of this rule a 'faceoff' must be made ten feet in front of goal with no players except the goal-keeper standing between the faceoff and the goal line."

6 "The carrying of sticks above the height of the shoulder is prohibited and shall be penalised with a minor penalty."

7 "A minor penalty shall be imposed on a player who lingers, or 'loafs' in the 'attacking' zone when the play is being carried in the other direction."

8 "All referees and assistant referees shall be garbed in blue trousers and white sweaters with the League monogram on the sweater."

9 "There shall be one umpire at each goal, who shall be appointed by the President of this League. . . . In the event of the goal being claimed, the umpire of that goal shall decide whether or not the puck has passed between the goal posts and entirely over the goal line, his decision simply being 'goal' or 'no goal.'"

10 "If, after the commencement of a match, it becomes apparent that either umpire, on account of partisanship, or any other cause, is guilty of giving unjust decisions, the referee may appoint another umpire to act in his stead."

CONACHER

1 No fewer than five Conachers played in the NHL, and three have been inducted into the Hockey Hall of Fame. Lionel and Charlie are the only brothers who *both* had sons go on to play in the NHL (Lionel's son Brian and Charlie's son Pete), and a third brother, Roy, also played but had no children who inherited his on-ice abilities. All three brothers are Honoured Members at the Hall. For virtually every year from 1925 to 1972, there was at least one Conacher playing in the NHL.

HEWITT

2 Long before Foster Hewitt called a game from the gondola at Maple Leaf Gardens, his father, William Hewitt, was creating the foundation upon which the game would develop the majority of its players. William was associated with amateur hockey in Canada for nearly sixty years and was manager for three of Canada's Olympic hockey teams, all gold medals. As was common in his day, he combined an active business in the game with newspaper writing and was editor of the *Toronto Star* for more than thirty years. He and famous son Foster have been inducted into the Hall of Fame, and Foster's son Bill took over as television voice for the Leafs toward the end of Foster's career.

HEXTALL

3 A three-generation hockey family, the Hextalls began with Hall of Famer Bryan, who played 12 years with the Rangers, 1936–48. Two of his sons, Bryan Jr. and Dennis, made it to the NHL, and Bryan Jr.'s son Ron was a longtime Philadelphia goalie. There has been a Hextall in the league for the past 33 years.

HOWE

4 It's one thing to send a son on to play in the NHL, and quite an accomplishment to send two sons, but to *play* with two sons in the NHL is something only Mr. Hockey could possibly have accomplished, in 1979–80, his thirty-second year of pro hockey. Gordie, Mark, and Marty played a total of 48 NHL seasons, not including their 18 combined years in the WHA. They are the only father-sons combination to play together in pro hockey.

Ron Hextall

5 NORRIS

None of the Norrises played hockey, but James and his three children — Bruce, Marguerite, and James Jr. — were involved in the game in the United States for decades. James Sr. bought the Detroit franchise and renamed it the Red Wings; the team won three Stanley Cups in the late thirties and early forties. With his children, he briefly controlled not only Detroit and the Olympia but the Chicago Stadium and Madison Square Garden. Co-owner Marguerite was the first woman to have her name on the Cup when the Wings won three more Cups in the 1950s.

6 PATRICK

One of only two families to have been represented by three generations in the NHL, the Patricks began with Lester Patrick and brother Frank. Frank won the Stanley Cup with the Vancouver Millionaires in 1915 and went on to coach and manage in the NHL, introducing many innovations and rules into the game while Lester managed the New York Rangers for many years. Two of Lester's children, Lynn and Muzz, went on to play in the NHL, and two of Lynn's sons, Glenn and Craig, also played.

7 SUTTER

The most famous family from Viking, Alberta, six Sutter brothers played in the NHL — Brent, Brian, Darryl, Duane, Rich, and Ron. All told, they have played 80 seasons in the NHL, almost 5,000 games and nearly 600 playoff games. Four of the Sutters were captains of their team (only Rich and Duane weren't), and so far two have become coaches, Brian and Darryl.

1 KAREN BYE

One of the brightest stars of women's hockey in the 1990s, Bye helped the U.S. team win silver at the 1992, 1994, and 1997 World Championships. In 1994 she earned a place on the tournament all-star team. Blessed with a superior shot, Bye scored five goals in six matches while helping Team USA win the inaugural Women's Olympic competition at Nagano in 1998.

2 CAMMI GRANATO

The sister of NHL winger Tony Granato, Cammi represented the U.S. at four World Championships in the 1990s. In 1998 she captained the Olympic Team to gold at Nagano. She scored eight points to tie for the team scoring lead while earning respect for her leadership qualities. Granato has been one of the most influential figures in expanding the popularity of women's hockey in the U.S.

3 GERALDINE HEANEY

A solid defender with superior offensive talent, Heaney won a World Championship with Canada in 1990, 1992, 1994, and 1997. She was a stalwart when the squad won the silver medal at Nagano. Heaney was voted the top blueliner at the 1992 and 1994 World Championships and has emerged as one of key leaders on the national squad.

4 MARIAN HILLIARD

During the 1920s, the University of Toronto iced some of the top women's hockey teams in the country. Their star performer was unquestionably Marian Hilliard, who grafted supreme play-making skills on to her natural skating ability. Hilliard's star shone brightest in 1924 when she led Varsity to victory over the highly acclaimed Ottawa Alerts in a two-game total goals series. This match was one of the first to draw attention to women's hockey.

ABBY HOFFMAN

5 Hoffman became a pioneer in female hockey when, as a youngster, she played in the Toronto Hockey League in the 1950s when most spectators were unaware she was a girl; Hoffman excelled on defence before moving on to other sports. Her place in the evolution of the women's game was acknowledged when the first Abby Hoffman Cup was presented to the Canadian champions in 1982.

ANGELA JAMES

6 James was one of the greatest forwards in the history of women's hockey. Her offensive talent was crucial to Canada's four World Championships between 1990 and 1997. She was particularly lethal at the 1990 tournament in Ottawa with 11 goals. James also excelled at the 1992 championship in Finland, when she earned a place on the tournament all-star team. Her exclusion from the 1998 Olympic team caused a major stir in hockey circles.

Angela James

7 HAZEL MCCALLION

Before gaining fame as the mayor of Mississauga, Ontario, Hazel McCallion was one of the top female players in the 1940s. A swift skater with a tenacious work ethic, the native of the Gaspé starred in a Montreal Women's hockey league during World War II. She served as the honorary chairperson at the first Women's World Hockey Championships in 1987, when the McCallion World Cup was presented for the first time.

8 HILDA RANSCOMBE

Ranscombe was the talented leader of the Preston Rivulettes club which dominated women's hockey in the 1930s. While leading her team to greatness, she formed the first great female forward line with Marm Schmuck and Gladys Hawkins. The powerhouse Rivulettes enjoyed a dynastic period unrivalled in the game by compiling a 348–2 record from 1930–39.

9 MANON RHEAUME

Rheaume became the best-known female player in the world in the early 1990s. She suited up for the QMJHL's Trois Rivières Draveurs in 1991–92, then the IHL's Atlanta Knights, and the NHL's Tampa Bay Lightning in a pre-season game the following year. Rheaume was an all-star when she helped Canada win gold at the 1992 and 1994 World Championships. She also represented her country at Nagano.

10 ERIN WHITTEN

Netminder Erin Whitten started the 1993–94 season with the ECHL's Toledo Storm. On October 30, 1993, she became the first female to record a victory in a professional match. Whitten backstopped the U.S. to the silver medal at the 1992, 1994, and 1997 World Championships. She was chosen top goalie at the 1994 tournament and starred when the team captured gold in Nagano in 1998.

A Dozen Of The Most **MEMORABLE**
QUOTES Of All Time

1

FOSTER HEWITT

The most famous broadcaster of them all coined three of the most memorable quotes in the history of the game. The first is his simple description of a goal: "He shoots, he scores!"

2

The second is his radio introduction to all his Maple Leaf broadcasts: "Hello hockey fans in Canada and the United States and Newfoundland."

3

And the third is his call of the most famous goal in the history of the game, Paul Henderson's game-winner in Moscow, September 28, 1972, to give Canada an historic win over the Soviet Union in the eight-game Summit Series. "Henderson has scored for Canada!"

4

MIKE PALMATEER

A quirky left-handed goalie for Toronto and Washington, Palmateer was as quick with a joke as he was with his glove. In the spring of 1979, the Leafs went to the quarterfinals, beating Atlanta two games to none in the first round of the playoffs, then facing Montreal. In the third game of the series, played at the Gardens with Toronto trailing 2–0 in the series, Cam Connor of the Habs scored a lucky goal on his first shift of the game, 5:25 into the *second* overtime period. After the game, Palmateer declared: "That's one thing I can't do — stop someone who doesn't know what he's doing."

5

HARRY NEALE

Although famous in the 1990s as a broadcaster, Neale was for years a not particularly successful coach and then GM, mostly with the Canucks. During one agonising losing streak, Neale remarked dryly, "We're losing at home and we're losing on the road. My failure as a coach is that I can't think of anywhere else to play."

6 Neale once appeared on a post-game interview with the inimitable Dick Beddoes, who was loud and brash, and whose sartorial habits were colourful and highly lacking in coordination. Neale was coaching the Canucks at a time when they had uniforms with the ugly black and yellow "V" as a crest, and Beddoes caustically commented that they were the worst sweaters in the league. He asked Neale where they got those hideous sweaters. Neale responded, "We consulted your tailor, Dick."

BOB JOHNSON

7 A true hockey coach and lover of the game, Johnson was one of the most successful bench bosses the United States has ever produced. His excitement was effusive and contagious, and his most famous declaration is still repeated by many lovers of the game no matter what the day or season: "It's a great day for hockey."

To which Glen Hanlon, NHL goalie, rebutted, "If you're a goalie, it's never a great day for hockey."

HAROLD BALLARD

8 The dictatorial owner of the Leafs signed the first Swedish-trained players for the NHL, future Hall of Famer Borje Salming and not-so-successful winger Inge Hammarstrom. While Inge had skill and speed and grace, his play along the boards and in the corners was timorous at best, and led Ballard to comment: "He could go into the corner with six eggs in his pocket and not break one."

DARRYL SITTLER

9 The night of February 7, 1976, was the most successful single night an NHL player has ever experienced in one game. Darryl Sittler of the Maple Leafs scored ten points (six goals and four assists) against the Bruins and their back-up goalie, Dave Reece. Reece never played another game in the NHL, and later Sittler quipped about how the goalie might have reacted to the career-ending night: "He was so upset, he tried to kill himself. He jumped onto train tracks, but the train went through his legs."

10 CONN SMYTHE

The most famous and successful owner in the history of the game, Smythe built the Leafs and Maple Leaf Gardens and created a tradition and dynasty that are part of the game's ongoing history. One of his philosophies about the game remains, to this day, an axiom for many hockey men: "If you can't beat 'em in the alley, you can't beat 'em on the ice."

11 RON WILSON

During a playoff game between Anaheim and Detroit in 1996 at the Joe Louis Arena, Ducks coach Ron Wilson became increasingly irate at the calls referee Kerry Fraser was making against his team. During a break in the action, he called Fraser to the bench and asked him who wrote *The Odyssey* and *The Iliad*. The confused ref asked his linesmen what that meant, and Ron Asseltine laughed and said, "Homer."

12 GORDIE HOWE

Howe appeared on the Dick Cavett Show in the 1970s, and Cavett wondered why hockey players always wore a protective cup but rarely a helmet. Howe answered, "You can always get someone to do your thinking for you."

PHOTO CREDITS

Acknowledgements

Jefferson Davis wishes to thank my wife Peggy and our children Ian and Julia for their love, support, and inspiration; my parents for giving me everything over the years; and my grandparents for their support and babysitting. Thanks also to Ron Ellis for his friendship and knowledge, and Jane Rodney, Phil Pritchard, and Craig Campbell of the Hockey Hall of Fame Resource Centre for all their help.

Andrew Podnieks would like to thank those who had a hand in getting the writer to the publisher and the book to the printer. To Jack David, Jen Hale, Wiesia Kolasinska, and Mary Bowness, and everyone else at ECW. To Tania Craan, for designing these simple pages with imagination and élan. To Peter Jagla for key inspiration down the homestretch with suggestions that were both mutated and mutilated to serve the author's own purely selfish, self-fulfilling ambitions with complete disregard to Peter's needs.

To those at the Hockey Hall of Fame who are forever supportive, notably Phil Pritchard, Craig Campbell, Darren Boyko, Jane Rodney, Jacqueline Boughazale, Tracey Greene, Izak Westgate, Dave Sandford, and, in absentia, author Sophie Harding. To Jon Redfern and Geri Dasgupta, as always. To rookie includees Liz, Ian, Zack, and number four, for patiently playing game after game. And to mi madre, leader of the focus group.